Holy Women Icons

Angela Yarber

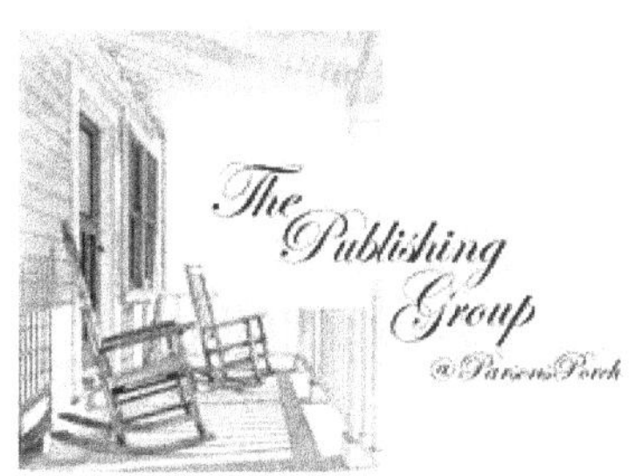

Parson's Porch Books

Holy Women Icons

ISBN: Softcover 978-1-936912-19-3

To order additional copies of this book, contact:

Parson's Porch Books
1-423-475-7308
www.parsonsporch.com

Parson's Porch Books is an imprint of Parson's Porch & Company (PP&C) in Cleveland, Tennessee. PP&C is an innovative non-profit organization which raises money by publishing books of noted authors, representing all genres. All donations from contributors and profits from publishing are shared with the poor

Dedicated to Lindsey.

You have given us more holiness than we could have ever imagined.

Acknowledgments

Holy Women Icons wouldn't be a book without first being a series of paintings. So, I am grateful for those galleries that have hosted them: Shell Ridge, Karma, Blue Lotus/Woven Soul, and Barnhills. I'm also tremendously grateful for all the people who have supported my art by purchasing or commissioning an original icon or buying a print. It means a great deal for someone to find enough value in my paintings to actually hang them in their home. The fact that these Holy Women are scattered all over the world, providing inspiration for friends, family, colleagues, and strangers is a gift.

And these paintings would have never been written about had Xochitl Alvizo not invited me to become a regular writer on *Feminism and Religion*, featuring one icon each month and expounding upon her story. Xochitl would not have discovered these paintings if Kittredge Cherry had not interviewed me about my beloved queer saints on *Jesus in Love*. So, I am grateful to these two women who have helped my icons find voices in the wider public. And I am grateful to the *Feminism in Religion* community for offering encouragement, constructive feedback, and inspiration along the way.

It was not until after the paintings, the exhibitions, the purchase and commission of icons, and writing about them for *Feminism and Religion*, that the possibility of this book became a reality. I published a previous book, *The Gendered Pulpit*, with Parson's Porch, but when I began exploring the possibilities of publishing *Holy Women Icons* I wasn't sure if it would be the right fit because of the large quantity of color images needed. I am so glad I addressed these concerns with David Russell Tullock, who has become a trusted colleague and friend. He had no doubt that *Holy Women Icons* was perfect for Parson's Porch and I couldn't be more pleased given their admirable mission of "turning books into bread." As a 501c3 publishing house who donates profits to feed the hungry, I feel confident that the holy women featured in this book would be honored to be a part of such a noble cause.

Finally, I am grateful for the holy women who fill my life: Wendy, Melissa, Trisha, Jen, Jen, Sharon, Patricia, Marybeth, Cindy, Jill, Lisa, Amy, Hillary, Ashley, Lisa, Kristin, Susan, Margaret, Lindsey, mom, and Elizabeth. Those final three holy women deserve particular gratitude. For my mother, thank you for not only teaching me that women can be and do anything, but for modeling this lived feminism in your life. As an ordained minister who studies, teaches, and writes about the holy, I thought I knew a little something about holiness. It wasn't until Lindsey entered into my life that I began to truly grasp how holy life can be. Thank you for giving us new life and expanding our family from two to three. I have experienced nothing more holy than holding our baby in my arms and that experience would not have been possible without you. And for my baby's other mommy, I cannot say thank you enough. Elizabeth is a holy woman because she is compassionate, gentle, brilliant, beautiful, silly, virtuous, and makes me a better person, while simultaneously making me laugh. I am well aware that my icons are not everyone's "style" of artwork, and I am particularly grateful that when they are not sold or hanging in a gallery, you welcome them into our home, transforming our hallways into explosions of color, as a gaggle of unlikely saints share their hearts with us. I'm lucky to share my heart with you. Thank you.

Table of Contents

Introduction

It began in the winter of 2010. I painted a triptych of Sophia for a Lenten exhibition. Inspired stylistically by the art of Shiloh Sophia McCloud and He Qi, I endeavored to give traditional iconography a folk twist in an attempt to make it more accessible, perhaps a bit less brooding and intimidating. Emboldened by the works of myriad feminist scholars in religion, my icons aimed to subvert traditional—and often patriarchal—depictions of a virtually all-male sainthood. Though there are surely some women depicted in iconography in the Catholic and Orthodox traditions of Christianity, and a robust number of women and goddesses in Hindu iconography, I found myself at a loss when it came to positive, affirming, and empowering icons of women and queer saints across the vast spectrum of religious and spiritual traditions.

With these things in mind, I decided that painting such icons would become my Lenten discipline. I would choose six women, research their lives and stories, and paint them, giving traditional iconography a folk feminist twist. Once the six week season of Lent ended, I realized that there were far more holy women than I had created. Thus began a new life-long project: Holy Women Icons.

In the future, I envision painting many more Holy Women Icons: Pauli Murray, Aurora, Terpsichore, Kalypso, Aphrodite, Oshún, Lucy Stone, the Grimké sisters, Isis, Venus, Judith, Yemaja, Mary Magdalene, Tara, Ruth St. Denis, Kali, Shekhinah, Eve Ensler, Harriett Tubman, and so many others. With all of my current icons and all the potential future Holy Women, I give traditional iconography a folk feminist twist.

Yet there are elements of traditional iconography that I wish to continue. Not only is the process of making an icon a spiritual discipline, sometimes even an act of worship, but the icon itself becomes an object of veneration for viewers. The icon is not an idol, but it does represent the holy in ways that remind worshipers of the virtues of their tradition. In the case of my Holy Women Icons, painting each one was surely a holy experience. And it is my hope that viewers may gaze upon them and be inspired to look inward to see how one might develop the virtues the icon bestows. How might I be more compassionate? How might I work more fully for justice? How might I affirm my own bodily existence? How might I celebrate the diversity and holiness of others? Each Holy Woman evokes such questions. Accordingly, I provide Questions for Contemplation with each icon. May these questions guide you to look both inward in an act of self reflection, and outward to determine how you might better engage the world with actions of justice, peace, compassion, and inclusion.

Far from complete, my Holy Women Icons stem from history, literature, scripture, mythology, the arts, dance, and personal relationships. "Most are uncanonized by the church," notes Kittredge Cherry in an interview about Holy Women Icons, but my "paintbrush consecrates them to become unconventional saints whose lives inspire people with new models of holiness ("Artist Paints Holy Lesbians and Other Women," on *Jesus in Love Blog*, March 1, 2012)." I am a strong believer in the sentiment: "if you can't see it, you can't be it." It is for this reason that I am a preacher. It is for this reason that I earned a Ph.D. It is for this reason that I paint. I do these things because of the many women and LGBTQ persons who have never seen a preacher who was one of them, a scholar who was one of them, or a painting that depicted them. And I think it is past time for feminist and queer theory to work together. My art is one way I put these theories into practice. It is my way of giving voice to persons and communities whose stories are rarely heard. Homiletics scholars Mary Donovan Turner and Mary Lin Hudson propose that "When a person who has been oppressed and silenced stands and speaks, that person experiences redemption (Turner and Hudson, *Saved From Silence*)." By painting these women and calling them "holy," it is my hope that I am contributing to their redemption and to the redemption of women and queers. In these ways, I see my paintings, much like my preaching, as a redemptive act.

Though not all of my icons are historical figures, their stories, myths, and narratives have been an important part of the lived histories of countless women from across cultures, faith traditions, and generations. Julius Lester contends that "History is not just facts and events. History is also a pain in the heart and we repeat history until we are able to make another's pain in the heart our own." Before saying more about this heart history, it is important to offer a few caveats regarding feminist spirituality.

In painting these women—many of whom have been tremendously oppressed—it is not my aim to appropriate their stories for my own gain. Many of their stories are so different from my own. For women like Jarena Lee, Anna Julia Cooper, Frida Kahlo, or Maya Angelou, I can never imagine or portray what it was like to live and work as a woman of color. But their stories and images are powerful, evocative, and must be shared. For figures such as Pachamama, Saraswati, or Guanyin, they are not a part of my own faith tradition or culture, but their stories and images are powerful, evocative, and must be shared. It is my hope that by writing this book and accompanying each icon with pieces of the powerful, courageous, and bold stories of these myriad women, I may shed light on some of the experiences of women that have been largely untold.

Cynthia Eller has named some of the problems with spiritual feminists (like myself) using and appropriating the images of women and goddesses from other cultures and traditions. Given that many spiritual feminists are white and often educated and middle class, it is easy for the movement to take images from oppressed traditions, whitewashing them into their own without acknowledging the depth of struggle and oppressions that reside inside many of these same powerful female images. By no means do I intend to imply that this is the case for *all* spiritual feminists. I think of the powerfully interdisciplinary work of Carol Christ and Judith Plaskow as examples of brave feminist forerunners who have paved pathways of understanding the role of goddess spirituality in ways that empower women, while also acknowledging the complexities of race, class, sexuality, and ability therein. It is my hope that my Holy Women Icons can do something similar. Eller highlights some of the power of images in feminist spirituality, saying:

> The use of imagery in feminist spirituality is intimately tied to and deeply expressive of the movement's theology. With their delight in images of the divine, spiritual feminists are saying things they feel cannot or should not be said with words alone. One of the central messages they are trying to communicate is that there was a time on earth when people worshiped goddesses in preference to gods, when the "feminine" was held to be sacred, and when women were accorded a greater social status than they enjoy now. (Cynthia Eller, "Divine Objectification: The Representation of Goddesses and Women in Feminist Spirituality," *Journal of Feminist Studies in Religion,* 24)

One additional problem that Eller highlights and that I seek to overcome with my own icons is the ways in which much of the imagery in feminist spirituality draws attention to essentialized elements of women's bodies. While nearly all feminists rage against Westernized popular culture's depictions of women's bodies that portray emaciated and often unattainable bodies, simultaneously glorifying the sexuality of breasts and hips, many spiritual feminists also draw attention to these elements of women's bodies. The intention is drastically different, but the visual imagery often quite similar. Breasts and hips are emphasized. In the case of patriarchal culture, these parts of women's bodies are *objects* of erotic gaze. In the case of feminist spirituality, these parts of women's bodies are *subjects* of a seemingly essential part of womanhood, birth, and the cycle of life.

There is no doubt in my mind that women from across cultural, racial, religious, and socio-economic lines are need of bodily affirmation, of knowing that their bodies are of deep value, worth, and beauty. These bodies come in all shapes and sizes, colors and hues. And feminist spirituality does a fairly good job of recognizing this. If our perception of these holy women impacts our perception of ourselves, it's important for the holy women to exemplify the beautiful rainbow of diversity of our world. Holy women come in every color, shape, size, and from a diversity of religions. They aren't just straight, white, and Christian.

In my folk feminist iconography I wanted to acknowledge the deep array of colors, hues, shapes, and sizes of holy women, but not by drawing attention to the specific parts of their bodies often essentialized as womanly or fertile. I did this to honor this deep array of bodily realities of women. Some women are naturally robust and curvy. Some women are naturally slim. Some women rejoice in the abilities of giving birth. And for some women the inability to give birth is a source of great pain. Still others see birth as not at all essential to their own womanhood. I also did this to honor those who may find inspiration and empowerment in the stories of these holy women, but whose bodily realities are gender queer. Breasts and hips do not empower everyone, after all. Breasts and hips do not a holy woman make.

The primary way my Holy Women Icons embody these notions is by making the heart of each woman the largest and most important part of the canvas. In most cases, the heart consumes the entire torso, illustrating that what dwells within the heart is more important than the breasts, stomach, or dissected and essentialized body parts. I affirm fully that all women's bodies are beautiful, worthwhile, and of deep value. But even more beautiful is the heart, what lies within. Returning to Julius Lester's sentiment of the historical heart is important here: "History is not just facts and events. History is also a pain in the heart and we repeat history until we are able to make another's pain in the heart our own."

By highlighting what I envision is within the hearts of these holy women, I hope that the pain of their hearts may become our pain. It is my hope that learning about the way many of these women have endured oppression, racism, sexism, slavery, homophobia, rape, violence, war, sacrifice, or the almost erasure of their existence, we may be emboldened to work to overturn these horrifying realities. We cannot forget these horrifying histories, no matter how much it pains our hearts. We cannot forget these women. We owe it to them to create a world where all may be surrounded by beauty and justice.

Above all, it is my hope that the icons and stories of these holy women will inspire you. I hope they will inspire you to acknowledge the holiness dwelling within your own heart. Honor it. Invoke it. Live it. More than that, it is my sincere hope that these inspiring women will embolden you to be an agent of revolutionary, inspirational, and courageous change in our world. May your heart be so filled with the beauty and pain of their stories that it seeps into your veins, limbs, and life in such a way that you will act to overturn systems of injustice and oppression, creating a world where all women—indeed, all of creation—may find the deep worth residing within.

Holy Woman Icon

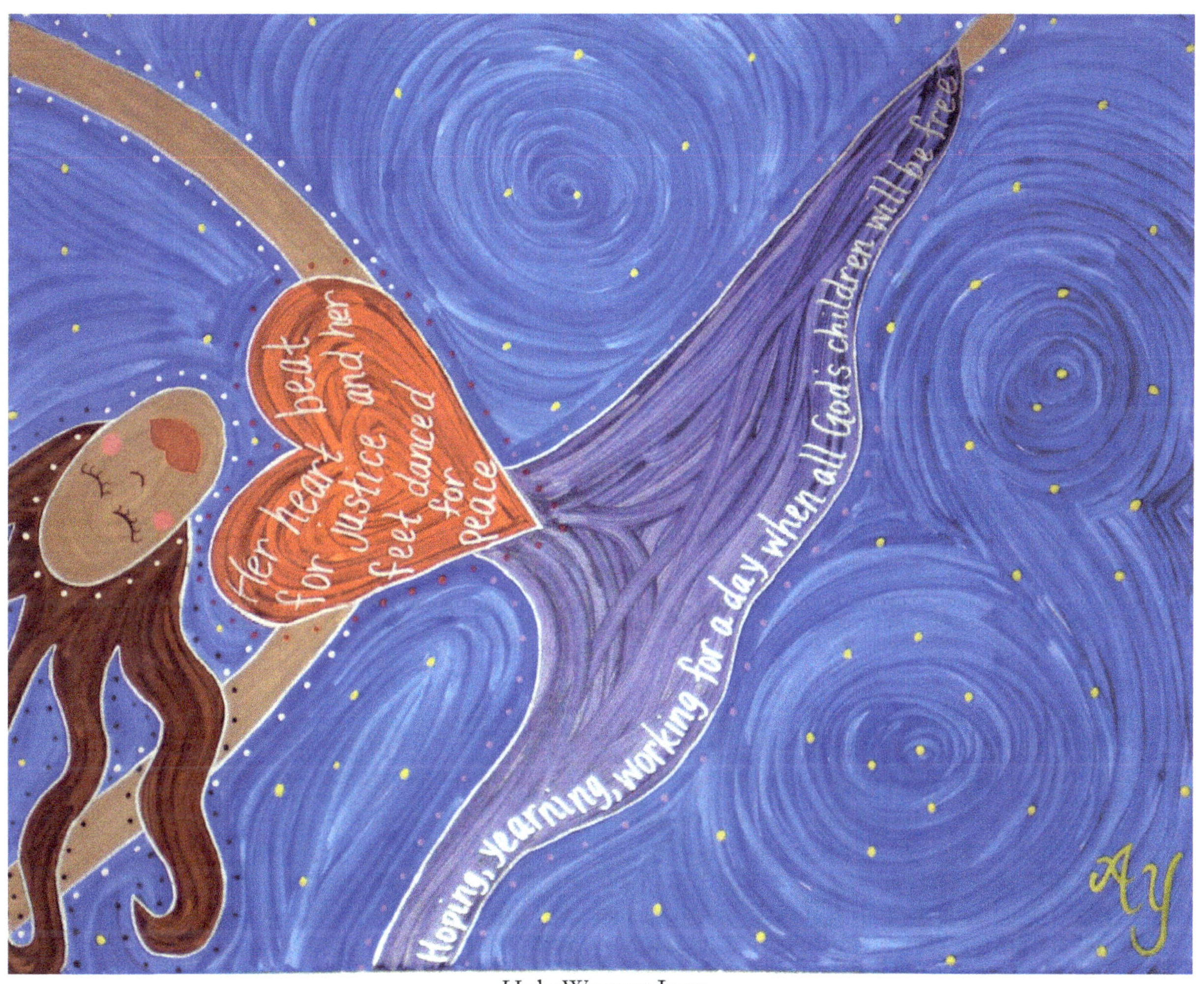

Holy Woman Icon
Acrylic on Canvas, 24x28

Holy Woman Icon

From this hour forward I ordain myself loos'd of limits and imaginary lines
-Walt Whitman

Many have claimed that artists are our contemporary prophets, those who rage against the status quo and call us to actions of justice that create beauty in the lives of all humanity, even all creation. So I turn to a great artist whose music has set free countless women and queer folk in search of new symbols, new language, new stories that are deep and wide enough to contain our subverted and searching spiritualities. The great womanist prophet, Tracy Chapman, sings these words in her song, *New Beginnings*:

We can break the cycle.
We can break the chain.
We can start all over.
In the new beginning
We can learn, we can teach
We can share the myths, the dream, the prayer.
The notion that we can do better
Change our lives and paths
Create a new world

And Start all over…

We need to make new symbols.
Make new signs.
Make a new language.
With these we'll define the world.

It is no secret that women, LGBTQs, persons of color, and myriad other oppressed groups have had to bear the brunt of oppressive religious symbols, signs, myths, and language. While many feminists rage within particular religious traditions to revise and redeem these symbols—linguistic and otherwise—many others have also stepped outside of tradition to create new symbols that have liberatory power for marginalized persons seeking to nourish their weary souls. Still others have combined these two seeming polarities by remaining within a faith tradition—often tangentially or on the fringe—and creating new liberatory symbols, as well. I've found myself dancing amidst all three of these modes of being as I paint my Holy Women Icons.

Some seek to revise and redeem the stories of women within particular faith traditions that have otherwise been drown amidst the torrents of patriarchy. I think of Mary, Guanyin, Jarena Lee, Saraswati, and Dorothy Day, for example. Some seek to step outside of tradition altogether and create new symbols: Mary Daly, Isadora Duncan, Frida

Kahlo. Still others, such as Tiamat, Baby Suggs, Fatima, and the Shulamite exist on the fringes of their tradition, creating new symbols and language to provide freedom for the oppressed and marginalized.

In an effort to create new symbols, new signs, new language, perhaps even new archetypes for women struggling to find their spiritual voice, I created Holy Woman Icon. In addition to painting these strong, bold, and powerful women who have subverted, revised, or revoked their faith traditions, I wanted to also create a holy woman, an archetype for who I strive to be as a queer feminist, a model for all women seeking to find their soul's voice. In imagining and then painting her image, I remind myself of who I want to be and become. In ordaining her into sainthood, I loose myself and all women of those imaginary lines that bind us.

Consequently, I cannot help but think of another prophet of our time, another artist who changes the status quo. Ntozake Shange's choreopoem and Broadway play, "For Colored Girls Who Have Considered Suicide When the Rainbow Is Enuf" concludes by bringing together all the different colors of women for a "laying on of hands" in which Shange evokes the power of womanhood as the Lady in Red begins reciting the often quoted line, "I found god within myself and I loved her fiercely." In this instance, Shange, like Chapman, creates a new symbol. For those of us steeped in religious language, one cannot help but think of the laying on of hands in ordination. By evoking this symbol, Shange revises what is otherwise an exclusive symbol—since women and queer folk are often excluded from ordained ministry—and revises it, redeeming the lived realities of women of color as holy, deserving of the fiercest of love.

As I laid my own hands on the canvas to paint this Holy Woman, I thought about Shange, Chapman, and I thought about hands. I thought of my own hands—hands that have laid on the heads of queer women in the act of ordination, hands that have held my baby, hands that have broken the bread and poured the wine in the act of communion, hands that have made love, hands that have repaired alternators and painted canvases, hands that have danced, comforted, and raised a fist in angry protest, hands that have, once upon a time, clasped together in prayers of anger, lament, and even praise. I thought of the hands of others in my life—hands that fed and nurtured, hands that hit and hurt, hands that gave and withheld, hands that embraced, and I thought of those hundreds of hands that laid upon my head some ten years ago, ordaining me to do something special, different, maybe even revolutionary.

With my hands on the blank canvas, which is larger than most of my other icons, I ordained this woman the archetype of holiness, arbiter of justice, embodiment of the divine, the manifestation of my calling. With her head thrown back in wild abandon, her arms thrust out embracing all creation, and her body dancing in the direction of freedom, Holy Woman Icon became an embodiment of Alice Walker's sentiment: "No one can end suffering except through dance." Virtually leaping off the canvas, prepared for a laying on of hands, her heart cries out to us:

Her heart beat for justice
And her feet danced for peace
Hoping, yearning, working for a day
When all God's children will be free

And this Holy Woman Icon invites us to place our hands on our hearts, ordaining ourselves loos'd of limits and imaginary lines, making new symbols, making new signs, making new language. With these we'll define the world.

Questions for Contemplation:
Turning Inward:
What virtues do you want to embody in your life?
Turning Outward:
How can you help other women be loos'd of limits and imaginary lines?

Anna Julia Cooper

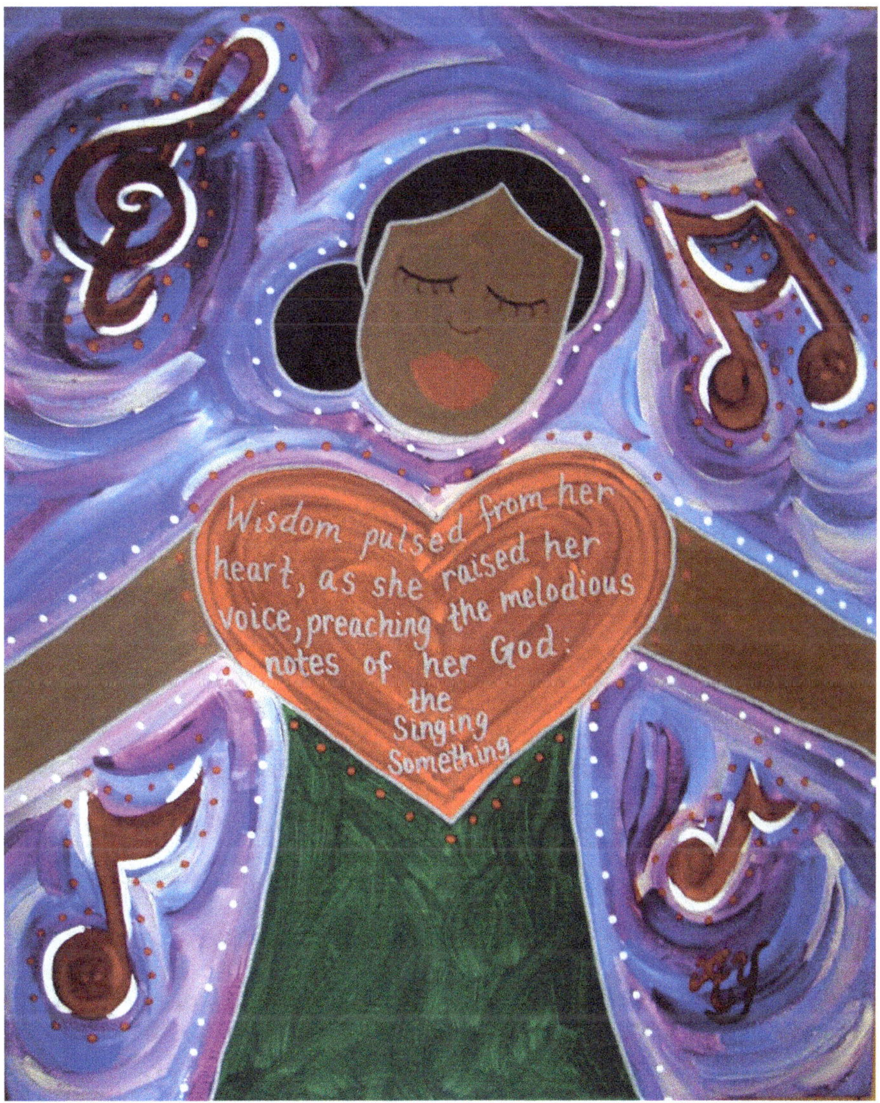

Anna Julia Cooper
Acrylic on Canvas, 16x20

Anna Julia Cooper

Anna Julia Cooper was born a slave in Raleigh, NC in 1858. Her mother was a slave and her biological father was her mother's white master. After living and working as a slave until the age of five, Cooper began her formal education at a school for slaves. She would grow up to become one of the most educated and intellectual black women of her century. In fact, she was the fourth African American woman to earn a Ph.D. in the United States, writing her dissertation on "Attitudes toward Slavery in Revolutionary France."

This holy woman also published a book entitled *A Voice from the South* in 1892. In her book, Cooper characterized God's likeness as a "Singing Something," a divine spark or "urge-cell" within each individual that, throughout history, has impelled humanity toward overcoming injustice into the full realization of freedom. She describes God as a liberating voice. This Singing Something within human beings is part of the "inborn human endowment" and "justifies the claim to equality by birthright" (Cooper, *Equality of Races*, 5). This Singing Something within human beings, then, is part of the very being of God.

Womanist theologian Karen Baker-Fletcher elaborates, saying, "In *A Voice from the South*...Cooper audaciously, shrewdly, and courageously questioned, challenged, and chastised the domination of the weak by the strong in Western culture. Originally, Cooper delivered most of the essays in this volume as lectures or speeches. She raised her voice to criticize the evils of racism, sexism, classism, and imperialism..." (Karen Baker-Fletcher, "Soprano Obligato," 173). Similarly, Mary Donovan Turner and Mary Lin Hudson laud Cooper as a preacher who held fast to her authentic voice, claiming that "through her love for music, Cooper came to use musical terminology to describe the importance of coming to speech. Blacks, she noted, were like a muffled chord. The black woman was a mute and voiceless note...Aware of the oppression that stifled their creativity and fullness, Cooper maintained that the black woman's 'little Voice' must be added to the chorus...For Cooper, then, being created in God's likeness is not imagistic. It is musical and auditory. Cooper understood our god-likeness to be in sound, words, voice. Thus, she spoke of not being created in the *image* of God, but in the *sound* of God." (Mary Donovan Turner and Mary Lin Hudson, *Saved from Silence*, 93).

Cooper's bold voice rose, like the voices of many other strong black women who sang the history of survival embedded in spirituals and gospel music. With voices raised in lament, solidarity, and protest, we remember these songs that arose out of the Singing Something that dwells within...

"Nobody knows the trouble I've seen. Nobody knows but Jesus" speaks of the ways in which Jesus is the co-sufferer, the one who knows what it's like to be exiled, enslaved, and oppressed.

"Sometimes I feel like motherless child a long way from home" speaks of the ways in which slaves were ripped out of the context of home and family, literally separated from mothers, with the compassion of God alone as their heavenly mother.

"Steal away, steal away, steal away to Jesus. Steal away, steal away home, I ain't got long to stay here" not only speaks to how suffering, slavery, and exile will be relieved by-and-by in heaven, but it was also code for when slaves could literally steal away at night to the underground railroad. And where would they steal away?

Wade in the water, wade in water children. Wade in water; God's gonna trouble the water" speaks of not simply the waters of baptism and how God troubles those waters into places of equality, but the song also functions as a code that reminded slaves that when they steal away, they should steal away into the river where the master's hounds cannot pick up their scent and they should wade in the water toward freedom.

And these songs not only functioned to identify with the compassionate and co-suffering God *and* as codes for escape, but they also served to subversively and secretly indict their captors. *"Have ya got good religion? Certainly, Lord!"* not only speaks to the need of having good faith in the compassionate and co-suffering God, but it also indicts those who *don't* have good religion, who keep faith and freedom away from black Americans.

So, with musical notes swirling about her, Anna Julia Cooper stands strong, centered with her arms spread so wide that they reach off the canvas, embracing and emboldening us to find the Singing Something within, as her heart cries out to us:

Wisdom pulsed from her
Heart, as she raised her
Voice, preaching the melodious
Notes of her God:
The Singing Something

We remember, lament, and repent for the injustice and oppression white Americans have heaped upon black people throughout history. But we also remember, celebrate, and honor the bold, courageous, and prophetic voices of many black Americans in the midst of such oppression—in history and today. Anna Julia Cooper was one of these voices. Her songs, her scholarship, her preaching, and her prophetic witness may have occurred in the late 1800s, when black women were ostensibly treated as the least among us. Yet her songs, her scholarship, her preaching, and her prophetic witness remain with us still, reminding us of that urge cell within, the Singing Something, whose song is a song of freedom, a song of justice, a song of equality.

Questions for Contemplation:
Turning Inward:
How can you better honor the "Singing Something" dwelling within you?
Turning Outward:
How can you empower others to find the "Singing Something" inside their hearts?

Dorothy Day

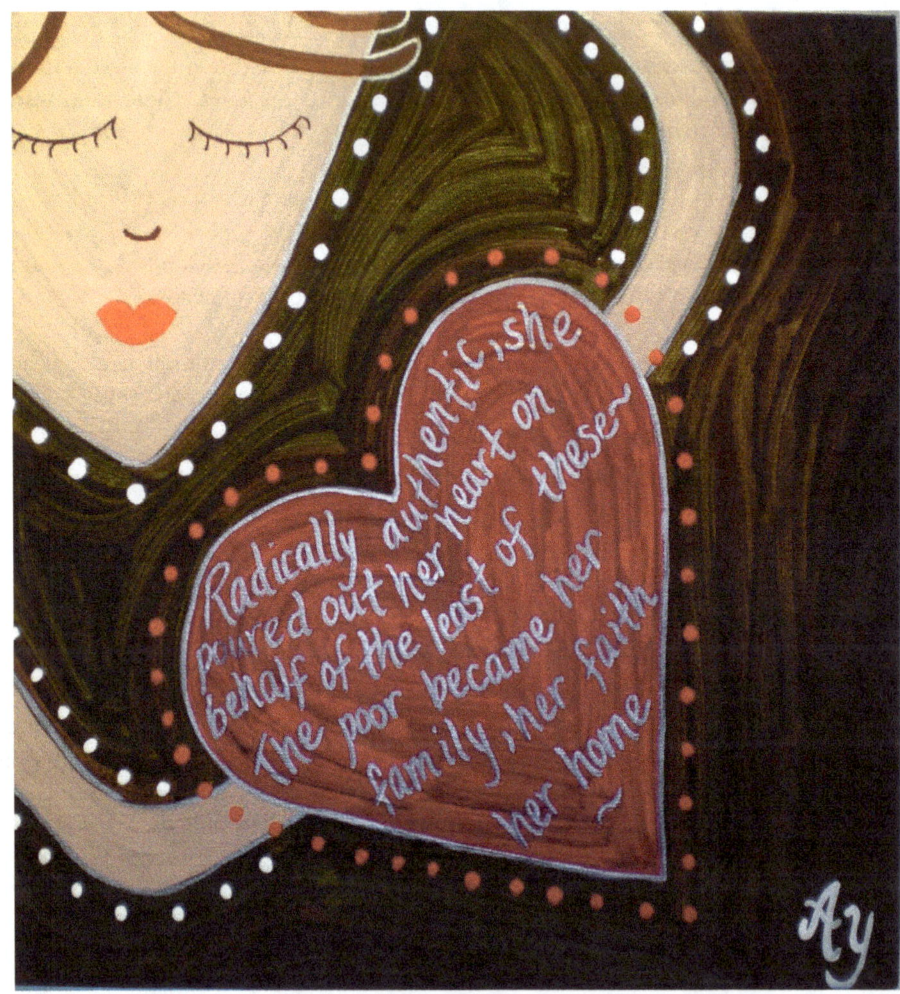

Dorothy Day
Acrylic on Canvas, 12x12, Ledbetter Private Collection

Dorothy Day

Radical Revolutionary. One with the workers. Daily works of mercy. One who challenged the status quo. She never wanted to be called a saint, though the Claretian Missionaries proposed that she be canonized in 1983. The Catholic Church calls her a "Servant of God." I call her a Holy Woman Icon. Born on November 8, 1897 Dorothy Day's radical spirit, her development of the Catholic Worker Movement, and her solidarity with the poor have taught countless women what it means to be a revolutionary. This American anarchist and activist converted to Catholicism as an adult after living what many describe as a bohemian lifestyle. She advocated the Catholic economic theory of distributism, daily works of mercy, pacifism, and solidarity with the poor.

She began her career as a journalist, writing for Socialist publications, such as *The Liberator, The Masses,* and *The Call.* She was rumored to say to other Socialists that she was "a pacifist even in the class war." Her radical stances on workers' rights and class warfare combined with progressive Catholic social teaching when she joined with Peter Maurin to establish the Catholic Worker Movement. The Catholic Worker Movement began with the publication of the *Catholic Worker* in 1933, admonishing progressive Catholic social teachings in the midst of the Great Depression and a pacifist position in the midst of war. The publication expanded to include houses of hospitality in the slums of New York City. These hospitality houses flourish all over the world today as intentional communities—urban and farm—where people live together communally, providing direct aid for the poor and homeless, while also advocating for nonviolent action on their behalf.

Throughout her life she was arrested numerous times for civil disobedience, always standing in solidarity with poor workers, sometimes participating in hunger strikes until justice was given. By the 1960s she was called the first hippie and a few years before her death in 1980 she joined Cesar Chavez in California to support his work to provide justice for farm laborers. In so doing, she was arrested with the other protestors at the age of 75 and spent ten days in jail.

As it did in life, her heart takes center stage on the canvas and she is surrounded by nary an embellishment, living and loving simply and truly, her heart crying out to us:

Radically authentic, she
Poured out her heart on
Behalf of the least of these—
The poor became her family, Her faith,
Her home

Radical Revolutionary. One with the workers. Daily works of mercy. One who challenged the status quo. These are all attributes I strive toward as a feminist. So, it's no surprise that on October 20, 2013 at 9:44am when a new life entered into our world, my wife and I chose to include the middle name "Day" on the birth certificate. Now there is one more squirmy, healthy, radical revolutionary in the world, weighing in at a robust 8 pounds and 6 ounces, with two mommies that are grateful for one brave woman who taught us what it means to offer mercy. Thank you, Dorothy Day. You may not be a saint, but you've certainly made our lives a bit more holy.

Questions for Contemplation:
Turning Inward:
What revolutionary sparks dwell within you?
Turning Outward:
How can you show daily works of mercy to others?

Georgia O'Keeffe

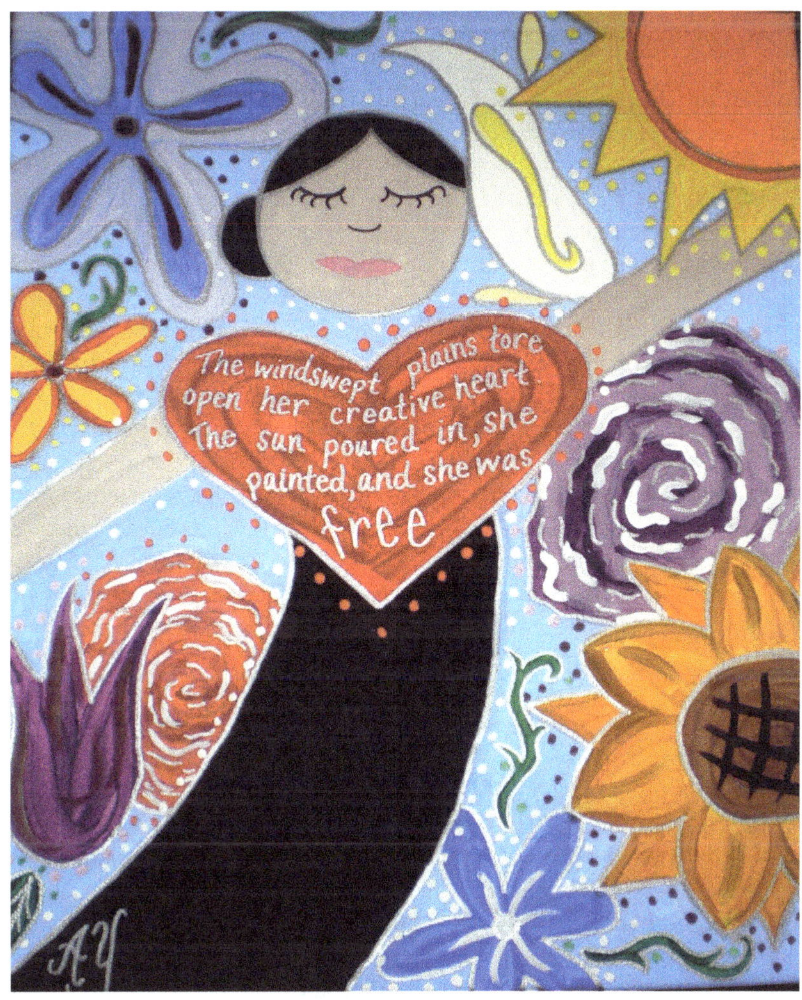

Georgia O'Keeffe
Acrylic on Canvas, 11x14

Georgia O'Keeffe

Hailed as the Mother of American Modernism, her seemingly vaginal flowers lauded by feminists and artists alike, Georgia O'Keeffe stands as a sentinel for strong, creative women who balk at tradition and embrace a faraway freedom. Though she adamantly denied any association with female genitalia embedded in her sensuously up-close-and-personal flowers—even from feminist artists as famed as Judy Chicago—she remained a female force unbound, painting, living, loving, and creating on her own terms.

Born in November 1887, O'Keeffe knew she would be an artist from the young age of seven. Whether you're familiar with her intricate flowers, soaring skyscrapers, or desert skulls depends largely on the period of her life that interests you. Whether it was the rural Wisconsin farm of her childhood, the bustling city of New York where she began her relationship with famed photographer Alfred Stieglitz, the peaceful lake in the Adirondack Mountains where they summered, or the harsh desert landscapes of New Mexico where she devoted her later years, she found inspiration and captured beauty wherever she lived, camped, traveled, hiked, or drove in her Ford Model A.

During her tumultuous relationship with Stieglitz, he photographed her hands, face, and naked body in such a way that made her person a recognizable icon just as much as the irises, ladders to the moon, and vast desert landscapes she painted so thoughtfully. Stieglitz may be partially responsible for her professional entre into the art world because he was the first to display her work—charcoal drawings—in his famous avant-garde gallery 291. She illustrated her staunch independence when she challenged her lover for showing her work without her official permission. From that moment on, she flourished as an artist who captured the feeling of a place more so than merely copying the place's image. Perhaps this is why countless other feminists have found inspiration and empowerment in her flowers, claiming that they embody the essence of woman. Fueling these feminists claims was also the fact that O'Keeffe often traveled to New Mexico with a female friend where the two hiked, camped, stripped naked in the Southwestern sun, and were rumored to have a lover's tryst in the faraway desert land. Needless to say, Stieglitz remained in New York City or the Adirondacks during these journeys.

When Stieglitz (who was 23 years her senior) passed away, O'Keeffe made New Mexico her permanent home, gathering stones, skulls, and flowers and shaping them into architectural still life paintings silhouetted against the expansive blue skyline. She was viewed as a fierce individualist who savored solitude and painted on her own in a time when women were expected to devote their lives to a man and his work. Clad in long black dresses, dark men's shoes, and her hair tied back into a tight bun, she appeared almost monk-like against the deep red rocks and sandy plains of the New Mexico backdrop. In her solitary attire, she braved the wild desert—the "faraway" as she called it—claiming, "I've been absolutely terrified every moment of my life—and I've never let it keep me from doing a single thing I wanted to do."

It was in this deserted landscape where she found true freedom, her heart ripped open so that the sun could shine in, filling her life and her art with light, hope, and a deep sense of adventure. So, surrounded by the flowers that made her famous and the crystal blue sky that set her free, the sun shines on Georgia O'Keeffe, as her heart cries out to us:

The windswept plains tore
Open her creative heart.
The sun poured in,
She painted,
And she was free.

Whenever I find myself afraid of the "faraway" that lies beyond my vision, or concerned about what society says women should be and do, I think of Georgia O'Keeffe. Unbound, and with her eyes open to both the expanse and intricacies of the natural world, she emboldens me to take the next step and discover the freedom found in faraway beauty.

Questions for Contemplation:
Turning Inward:
What faraway places are you afraid of? How can you embrace this fear and find inspiration in the faraway?
Turning Outward:
How can you invite others into your own faraway places of freedom?

Guanyin

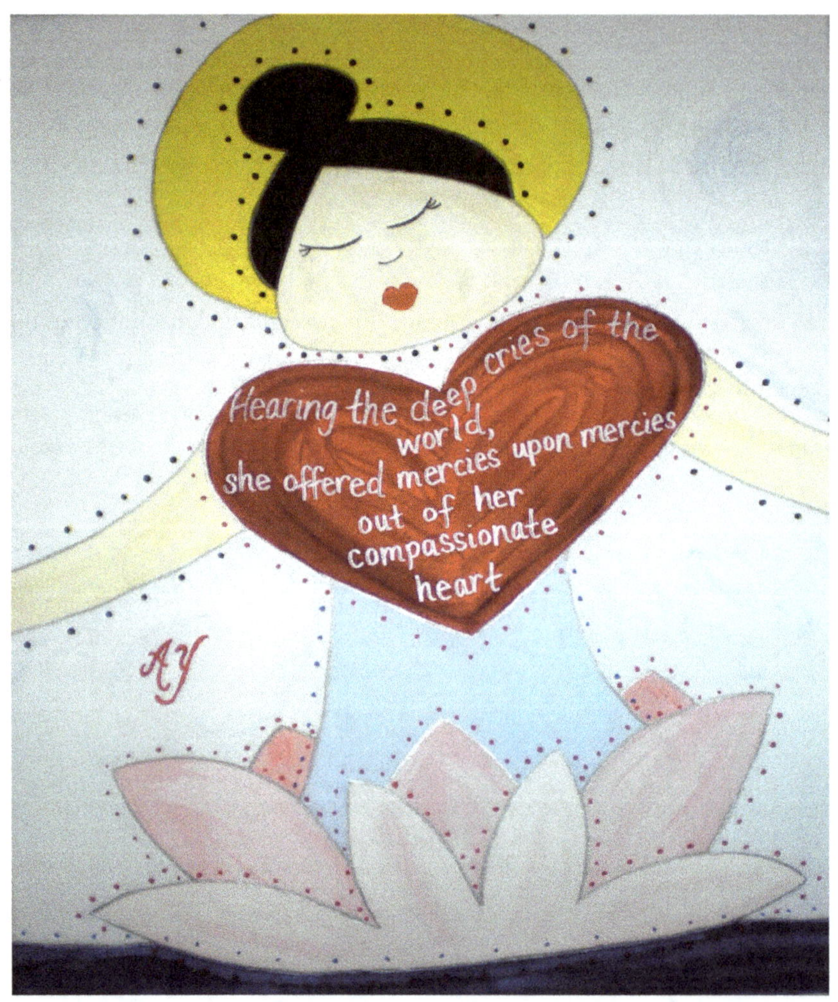

Guanyin
Acrylic on Canvas, 18x24

Guanyin

As we are bombarded with the injustice that surrounds on a daily basis, in the face of America's rape culture and as countless nameless victims are ravaged by war, poverty, racism, and violence, I sometimes find myself overwhelmed, as though my two hands are never enough to reach out, help, rage, change. And I find myself—and our world—in need of mercy and compassion. So, I am drawn to the Goddess of Mercy: Guanyin.

In English we know Guanyin as the Goddess of Mercy and Compassion. Generally regarded among East Asian devotees as originating from Avalokitesvara, her name is shortened from Guanshiyin, which means "One who hears the sounds/cries of the world." In the Lotus Sutra, Avalokitesvara is a bodhisattva who is androgynous and can take on the form of any female, male, adult, child, human, or non-human sentient being in order to teach the Dharma. Typically she is depicted in female form and she is widely venerated by East Asian Buddhists. Though she is particularly poignant for Buddhists, Guanyin is present in almost every facet of Chinese religion, from Buddhism to Taoism to shrines for local fishermen.

As the personification of compassion and kindness, Guanyin is sometimes seen as a mother-goddess and the patron of mothers. By the 12th century in China, her iconography was solidly female and in the modern period she is most often represented as a beautiful woman in a white robe or white dress.

She is a source of unconditional love, sometimes viewed as a savior who places the souls of those deceased into the center of a lotus flower. In her bodhisattva vows, Guanyin promises to answer the cries of all creatures and to liberate them. Because her compassion extends beyond humans and unto all creation, she is often associated with vegetarianism in East Asia. You may find a depiction of her looking downward at the earth so as see all the suffering of the world, standing on a lotus flower or dragon in many Buddhist vegetarian pamphlets, magazines, or Chinese vegetarian restaurants.

According to the *Complete Tale of Guanyin and the Southern Seas,* legend has it that Guanyin vowed to never rest until she freed all beings from samsara. No matter how hard she tried, she realized that there were too many beings that lacked fulfillment and that she was unable to save them all. After being overcome by the needs of the world, her head split into eleven pieces. So, when the Buddha Amitabha saw her despair, he gave her eleven heads so that she could have more ears to help her hear the pleas of those who are suffering. When she heard the cries of the universe and understood their suffering, she tried to reach out so that she could help all who were in need. But her two hands were not enough, so they shattered into pieces. Again, Buddha Amitabha witnessed her compassion and despair and gave her a thousand arms so that she could reach out to all who are in need. Like iconographic depictions of the Buddha, Guanyin is also sometimes depicted with webbed hands so that no one can slip through the cracks between her fingers. She, like the Buddha, can hold the suffering of all living creatures.

Whether she is portrayed as having eleven heads or one, a thousand arms or two, Guanyin is almost always surrounded by a halo of light, wearing white or light blue, and often accompanied by a lotus, dragon, or two young acolytes.

So, I spread her arms wide—wide enough to embrace and hold the entire world—and depicted her rising out of the lotus where she places the souls of those we have lost. She stands in solidarity with our suffering, as her heart cries out to us:

Hearing the deep cries of the world,
She offered mercies upon mercies
Out of her compassionate heart.

It's worth noting, too, that the act of compassion and feeling of mercy and love is viewed as *being* Guanyin. Therefore, a merciful, loving, compassionate, and kind individual is understood to *be* Guanyin. In the moments when we show compassion, when we share mercy with all sentient beings, we become the Goddess of Mercy. When we become Guanyin, one less suffering soul slips through the cracks and is instead held in compassionate embrace. Let it be so.

Questions for Contemplation:
Turning Inward:
How can you show more compassion to yourself?
Turning Outward:
How can you show more compassion to others?

Jephthah's Daughter

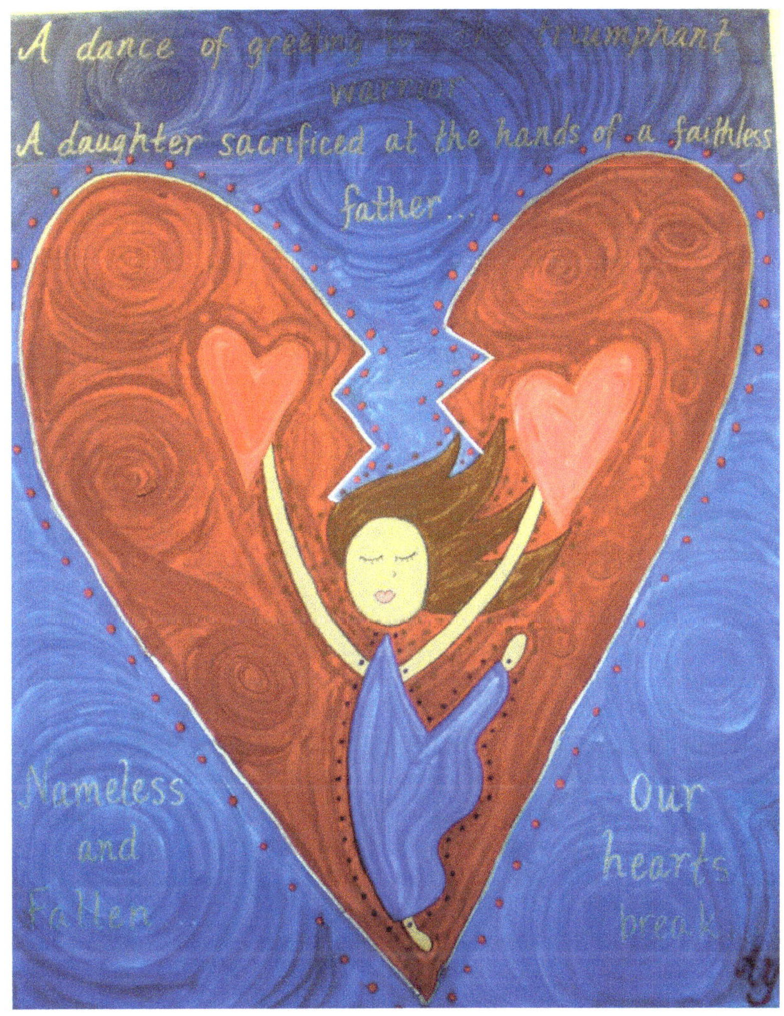

Jephthah's Daughter
Acrylic on Canvas, 16x20, Garber Private Collection

Jephthah's Daughter

And Jephthah made a vow to the Lord, and said, "If you will give the Ammonites into my hand, then whoever comes out of the doors of my house to meet me, when I return victorious, shall be the Lord's, to be offered up by me as a burnt offering…Then Jephthah came to his home at Mizpah; and there was his daughter coming out to meet him with hand drums and with dancing…he did to her according to the vow he had made…" (Judges 11:30, 34, 39)

When I was a little girl I used to make up routines to perform for my family. From Tina Turner's "What's Love Got to Do With It" to Michael Jackson's "Beat It" I can remember making up creative choreography and performing in front of the affirming audience that was my family. Often times, my routines were accompanied by props, such as a hula hoop, roller skates, or an unwilling younger brother. Whether I had props or not, there was always a big smile on my face as I twirled and leapt to the tunes on my family's 8-track, record, or cassette player. Half the fun was making up the routine and practicing until it was performance perfect. The other half of the fun was the response on my family's faces as I forced them to "watch me, watch me!" once again. Despite the cheesiness of my routines and my silly props, they watched with delight, clapped, and encouraged me to dance all the more. Such is the experience for many fortunate children: choreographing routines, drawing pictures, making up skits and plays, and practicing to make their parents proud.

It is these very aspects of childhood play that haunt the story of Jephthah's daughter in Judges 11. A little girl skips out of her house to perform her newest routine upon the return of her daddy; little does she know what fate awaits her. Jumps and twirls of greeting, celebration, and welcome-home evolve into a dance of lamentation for a life short-lived as Jephthah's daughter succumbs to the foolish promise of her faithless father.

Here we are confronted with what Phylis Trible calls a "text of terror." What are we to do with this tale of injustice that is in scripture? For generations, faithful readers have wondered what happened to Jephthah's daughter: what did it mean for him to "do to her according to the vow he had made"? Did he actually sacrifice his only daughter? Was she really given as burnt offering because of the vow Jephthah foolishly made in the midst of battle? Most feminist scholars agree on one issue: it is precisely the ambiguity that describes the sacrifice that is typical of the entire narrative. This ambiguity suppresses details about the sacrifice as a type of apology, a subtle justification of Jephthah's behavior. As in much of history, the mighty warrior prevails uncensored; the violence he perpetuated upon his only daughter stalks him very little.

There are several aspects of the text that are worth mentioning in order to develop a fuller understanding of what is actually going on the story and what it means for us today. We note that Jephthah's story exists in book of Judges. Jephthah is indeed a part of the downward spiral of judges over Israel. He is quite a character himself. He's rejected by his community, the son of a prostitute, and doesn't know who his father is. Yet, he is a good warrior and is selected to fight on Israel's behalf.

We read that the "spirit of the Lord is upon him." Even with God's spirit within, Jephthah still finds it necessary to bargain with God while in battle. He makes a public announcement in his hometown of Mizpah: "If God helps me win this war against the Ammonites, then I'll sacrifice whoever comes out of my house when I return from battle!" The word "whoever" is ambiguous, as well. We are left only to wonder if he is referring to the possibility of an animal sacrifice, but surely not his little daughter. Did Jephthah not remember that it was customary in ancient Israelite culture for women to dance out of their doorways with a dance of greeting and victory upon the return of men from battle? Did he not think about the possibility of his little daughter being a part of this noble custom?

So, Jephthah and the Israelites are victorious; they defeat the Ammonites. As he returns home, what is it that will exit the door of his house first? None other than his one and only child: his daughter, whose name the narrator did not find important enough to mention. She exits the house with a hand drum and with dancing. Just as other Israelite women were dancing out of their homes to greet fathers, sons, brothers, and husbands with greeting and celebration, so too, Jephthah's daughter skipped and danced forth to celebrate the return of the daddy that she probably missed. Perhaps she had been working on her routine, choreographing the steps, practicing on her hand-drum, and waiting for the perfect moment to praise her father for his victory.

The text tells us that she is his one and only child and that she is a virgin. In fact, three times in the passage we read that she has never slept with a man. This is important because it reminds us that she is the property of her father. In this time, women were owned by their fathers until they married; then they became the property of their husband. So, Jephthah's daughter was one of his only assets. Her loss would indicate a significant loss of property and his possible lineage. She had no children to carry on his name.

As this young child danced through the doorway, mindfully recalling her choreographed steps, prepared for her daddy's return, she did not know that her actions would "bring him low." She is probably quite shocked with his response to her dance. Instead of scooping her up and hugging her, praising her thoughtful gestures and beautiful dance steps, Jephthah rends his garments and yells at his little dancing daughter: "Daughter, why?! You are one with my enemies! For I have made a promise to God and I cannot take back my vow!" Why not, we wonder. Why can't you take back your silly vow? God does not require it.

And we wait for a voice from heaven to spare the dancing daughter. But, unlike Isaac, the child of promise, we hear no voice; a ram does not appear. God is silent. Her well-planned routines are replaced by the rending of garments: lamentation for the loss of lineage. Today let us rend our garments: lamentation for the loss of her name.

The story of Jephthah's faithless vow and his dancing daughter's demise stands as a paradigm for so many innocent victims that have suffered at the hands of proud people in power. This young daughter, who is not even awarded a name in scripture, is quite similar to the many who suffer injustices today. I think of the countless girls who have been victims of violence at the hands of faithless fathers. I think of persons and families caught in cycles of violence, nameless victims whose stories we never hear.

The story of Jephthah's daughter and her violent fate has been a part of my own story for quite some time. She occupies an entire chapter in my book, *Dance in Scripture: How Biblical Dancers can Revolutionize Worship Today*. I've preached about her on numerous occasions, created choreography in her memory, and hiked Mount Sinai to see the oldest depiction of her at St. Catherine's Monastery. I knew that she would be one of my Holy Women Icons. But this nameless daughter's story is different than all the others. Like Salome, she was only a child. Like Isadora, she died tragically. Like the Shulamite, Baby Suggs, Salome, Isadora, and Miriam, she danced. But we know their names. We don't know her name. And she died so violently, so young, so unnecessarily. So, when I spread my canvas to canonize her into sainthood, I knew she had to be different. Her heart must be broken; our hearts must be broken. The painting must be more childlike, as though it was painted by this innocent young girl and not by a professional artist. From this icon, Jephthah's nameless daughter's broken heart cries out:

A dance of greeting for the triumphant warrior
A daughter sacrificed at the hands of a faithless father
Nameless and Fallen…
Our hearts break

In order to be responsible feminists we must confront the injustices that surround us today. We must ask ourselves: who are those that are oppressed in my neighborhood? Who are those that are victimized in my country? Whose names do we not know in my community? Then we must ask: what can I do to change this cycle of oppression? How can we be an agent of change in an unjust world? It is our responsibility to mourn these tragic deaths, to dance their dances, and rend our garments with actions of justice and remembrance. Paint. Rend. Dance. Prophesy. Rage. We owe it to her.

Questions for Contemplation:
Turning Inward:
Have there been times in your life when your dances of greeting have morphed into dances of lamentation?
Turning Outward:
How can you prevent other girls and women from being sacrificed at the hands of foolish violence?

Lilith

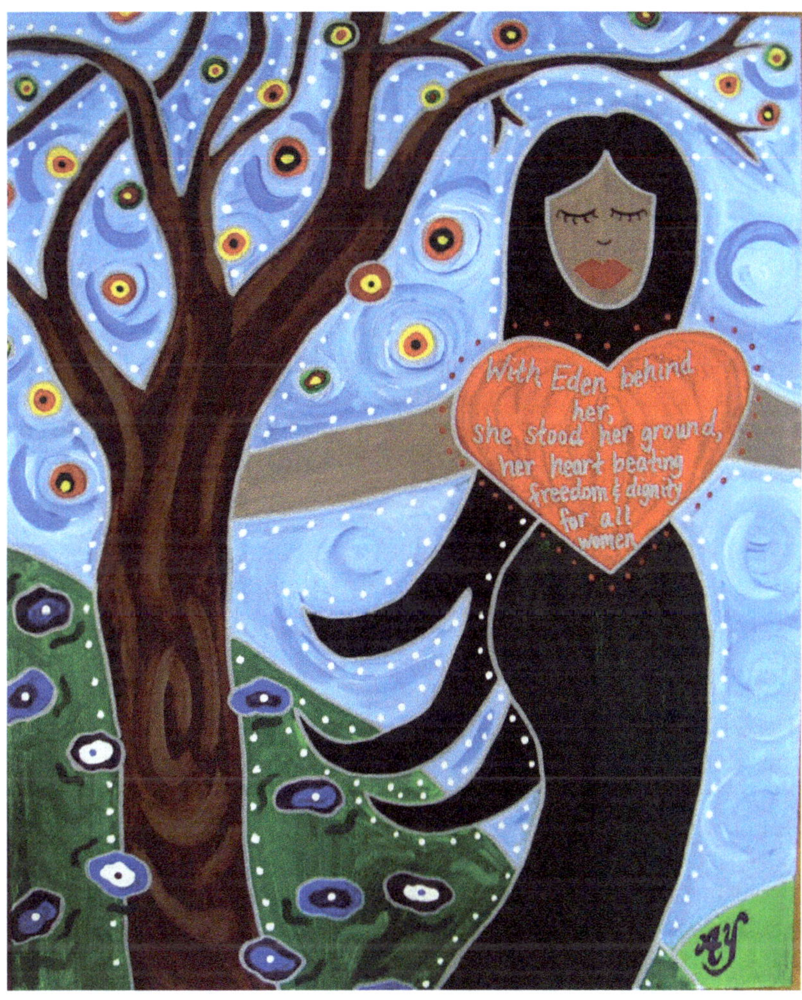

Lilith
Acrylic on Canvas, 16x20, Mercer Private Collection

Lilith

Lilith has been a misunderstood, appropriated, and redeemed woman throughout the ages. Many feminists claim her as an empowering figure in Jewish mythology, her story reclaimed by contemporary artists such as Sarah McLachlan, who created the all-women music tour, "Lilith Fair." Others have asserted that Lilith was a demon who seduced men and strangled children in the night.

Based almost entirely on Judith Plaskow's beautiful Midrash, "The Coming of Lilith," this holy woman has empowered me to reject the sexism and heterosexism that was rendering me broken. First, her story. Then—if I may—my own.

According to Plaskow's Midrash, God created Adam and Lilith from the same earth. Tired of Adam demanding that she be subservient to him, Lilith left the Garden of Eden. She was later befriended by Eve and her legacy of empowering women continues today.

Plaskow's powerful Midrash stems from a myth that has shifted over time. There is no single Lilith story, but many different stories must be sifted and sorted to determine who Lilith truly is and was. She appears explicitly only once in the Hebrew Bible (Isaiah 34:14) in a list of wild animals in desolate land. She is not described, but named simply: "Lilith." Some scholars surmise that the Lilith myth was so well-known by Isaiah's audience that there was no need to offer any explanatory words.

In Talmudic literature, Lilith is associated with the creation story in a manner similar to Plaskow's Midrash. Here she is also banished from the Garden. In the *Alphabet of Ben Sira* (7th-11th centuries) Lilith is presented as Adam's first wife. When she refuses to lie with Adam during sex, she calls out the name of god and flies away to an evil place filled with demons. By the end of the Talmudic period, the demonic and seductive elements of the Lilith myth were solidified. So, in the writings of the Kabbalah, Lilith is primarily understood to be a seductress and child-killer. Regarding this reputation, some feminist scholars assert that the vilification of Lilith intensifies over time because Lilith is perceived to be more and more powerful. The more powerful Lilith is perceived to be, the more evil her portrayal. What Plaskow's Midrash creates, redeems, and affirms is that Lilith left what was hurting and oppressing her and lived into who she was called to be: one who empowered women.

Like many other clergywomen, I had faithfully served the church for nearly fourteen years. After eleven years of ministry, I accepted a call to become Pastor for Preaching and Worship at a Baptist church after finishing my Ph.D. Upon hiring me, we became the only Baptist church in the country with two out lesbians as head pastors. My pulpit was free. My calling to justice, inclusion, and radical hospitality affirmed. I loved—and continue to love—the staff and the people who call this church home. I loved—and continue to love—preaching. But sexism and heterosexism have their way of creeping into the most unlikely of places. And the inner-workings of power and privilege make dealing with these "isms" ever more difficult.

Though the church would nary tolerate overt and blatant sexism or homophobia from within the congregation—and spoke out against the blatant forms I received in hate mail—microaggressive sexisms and heterosexisms continued to exist, flourishing in spaces we thought were safe, affirming, and progressive. Microaggressions are everyday slights, insults, or invalidations directed at marginalized groups—persons of color, sexual minorities, women, etc—by individuals who typically have good intentions and are decent, moral, thoughtful persons who may not be fully aware of their privileged positions of power. Psychologists who focus on cultural diversity issues claim that microaggressions build up over time, causing stress, pain, and anxiety for marginalized persons.

After months and months of trying to address these issues, my health continued to decline. I reread Barbara Brown Taylor's *Leaving Church* and I thought a lot about Lilith. How did she garner the courage to leave the "safety" of the Garden for the great unknown? I began to paint.

The colors of Eden filled my canvas, as a strong woman walked left, reaching out toward the unknown that lies beyond the Garden, the place she has called home. Lilith's heart cries out to us,

With Eden behind her,
She stood her ground,
Her heart beating
Freedom and dignity
For all women.

Not knowing what lies beyond the place I've called "home" for nearly fourteen years, I resigned from my position in a coveted, progressive Baptist pulpit. I proclaimed the Word in that pulpit one last time on July 14, 2103, preaching with my voice firmly set on freedom, insisting that all humanity be treated with dignity, equality, compassion, and beauty, knowing that my calling is to justice. No exceptions.

Since I offered my resignation many have asked me if I think the church—any church—can exist with*out* sexism and heterosexism. Called, ordained, degreed, and with over a decade dedicated to working to overcome it, I'm afraid my answer is a faint, but hopeful, "I don't know." The Garden—the church—can be a beautiful place. Like Lilith, I must climb over the Garden's walls and find out what's on the other side.

Questions for Contemplation:
Turning Inward:
What prevents you from climbing over the garden's walls and finding liberation?
Turning Outward:
How can you help tear down the walls that cage women into oppressive structures and cycles?

Sappho

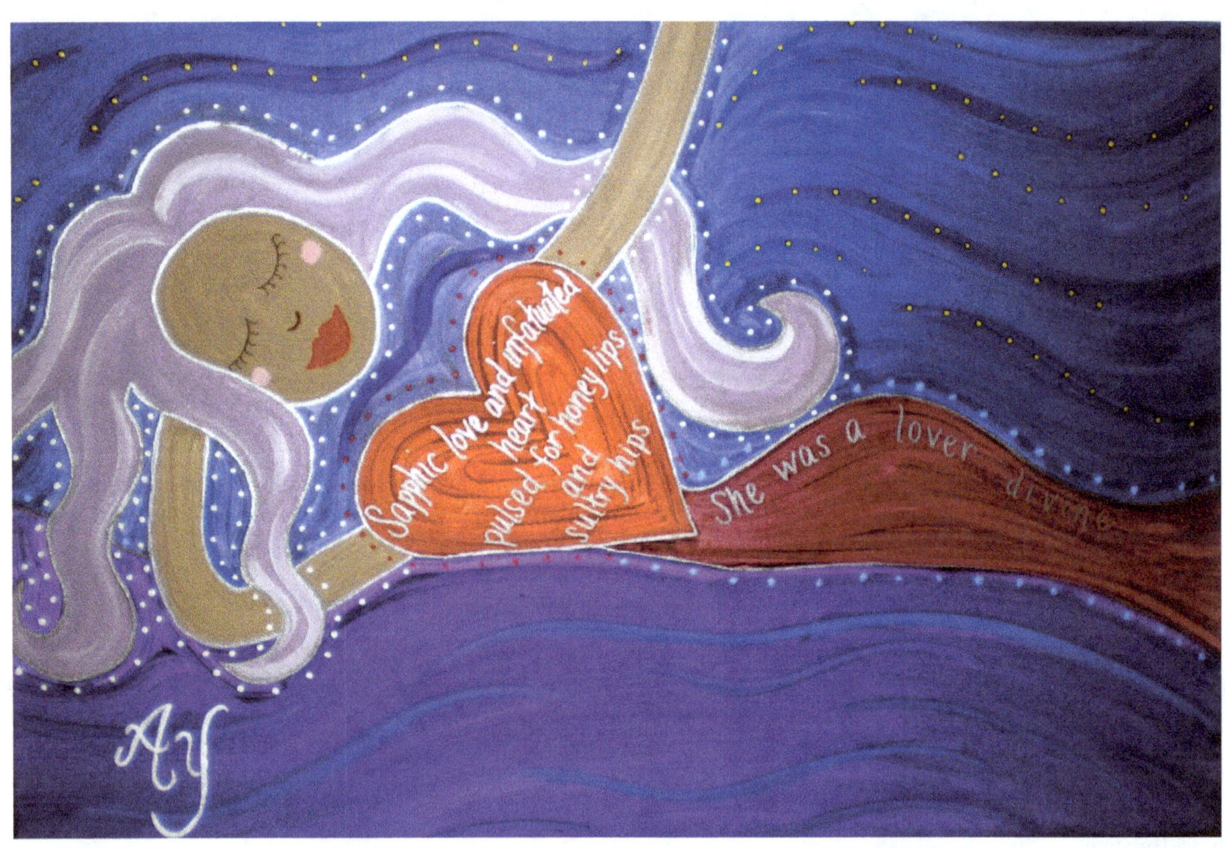

Sappho
Acrylic on Canvas, 24x36

Sappho

"Someone, I say, will remember us in the future," she once wrote. To my knowledge, she was never dubbed a prophet. A muse, yes. A romantic, perhaps. But never a prophet, rarely holy, and nary an icon. Until now. Hailed as one of the best Greek lyric poets, many have tried to forget her, or at least the more provocative elements of her life. The passionate poet Sappho was born on the island of Lesbos around 620 BCE (sometime between 630-612 BCE). The word lesbian stems from the place of her birth and her name is the origin of the word sapphic, though most scholars assert that little is known of her actual life and that the majority of her poetry is not autobiographical. Yet her lyric poetry speaks of love for both sexes and myriad people.

What is more, the idea of homo and heterosexuality are not transhistorical essences, but instead are relatively recent socio-historical constructs. To say that there were strict sexual binaries in the ancient world in which Sappho lived would be an anachronism. Sexuality was much more fluid. Not surprisingly, many scholars have tried to name and claim male lovers for Sappho, a heteronormative attempt to erase her fluid sexuality, her hope to be remembered in the future dashed, demeaned, forgotten. In fact, during the Victorian Era, many asserted that Sappho was the headmistress of a girls' school, another attempt to "straighten" out her memory, her poetry, her love.

In an interview with Kittredge Cherry, she asked how it was that I chose to include this seemingly un-saintly woman with the rest of my Holy Woman Icons. Sappho may not appear to fit in with all the others at first glance. I responded simply: "It is long overdue for LGBT persons to be affirmed and told their lives, bodies, and beings are holy and beloved. Painting Sappho, in all her beautiful and bodily wisdom, was my way of affirming and redeeming the love and life she represents. There are many ways to be holy. Her life and poetry is an example of this." Sappho, like all these Holy Women, deserves to be canonized in canvas.

So, when I began my Holy Woman Icons project, I knew that Sappho was among them. Her canvas is the largest of them all, filled with the lavender and purples that have described her. She lounges, longing, leaning, reaching. But it is not her seductive pose or disheveled hair that is central, but her heart. And her heart cries out to us, making us remember:

Sapphic love and infatuated
Heart
Pulsed for honey lips
And
Sultry hips
She was a lover divine…

We remember, Sappho. We remember.

While it is my sincere hope that my canvas and her sultry iconography evoke our memory, I find it important to highlight her own words. It is the best way to remember her, after all. Hear now, one of Sappho's most famous poems, *Prayer to Aphrodite:*

PRAYER TO APHRODITE

Eternal Aphrodite, Zeus's daughter, throne
Of inlay, deviser of nets, I entreat you:
Do not let a yoke of grief and anguish weigh
Down my soul, Lady,

But come to me now, as you did before
When, hearing my cries even at the distance
You slammed the door of your father's house—
Golden! and hastened

To harness your chariot. Then pretty sparrows
Drew you forthwith over the dark lands,
Beating their crisp wings. From the outer spheres,
Down through the inner,

Steeply they descended. At last you, Divine Lady,
Beaming your unearthly smile at me,
Asked was I in distress once again—for,
Why had I called you?

And what did my unruly heart demand
Of you now? "And whom do I urge this time
To return your generous friendship? Who,
Sappho, has been stubborn?

For if she avoids you, soon she will come
Knocking; if refuses presents, will shower them
On you; if she loves not, she shall love, and
Learn to be kinder."

I beg you, come. Free me from this oppression.
All that my heart longs to see accomplished,
Goddess, do it. No one could resist if you were
Fighting beside me.

(Sappho, "Prayer to Aphrodite," translated by Alfred Corn in *World Poetry: An Anthology of Verse from Antiquity to Our Time*, edited by Katharine Washburn, John Major, and Clifton Fadiman.)

Her legend, her poetry, evokes the memory—and present reality—of queer women's lives. Therefore, we can revel in the beauty of Sappho's words, poetic justice providing respite in an otherwise homophobic and patriarchal world. Here, in Sappho's stanzas, immersed in her poetic lines, we find beauty, affirmation, perhaps even redemption:

I beg you, come. Free me from this oppression.
All that my heart longs to see accomplished,
Goddess, do it. No one could resist if you were
Fighting beside me.

Come, Sappho, come, Aphrodite, so that we may free ourselves from all that binds and fight for love. Bold, prophetic, unabashed, never-ending, all-inclusive, sapphic love.

Questions for Contemplation:
Turning Inward:
How can you better honor the beauty and sensuality of your own body?
Turning Outward:
How can you better honor the beauty and sensuality of sexual minorities?

Baby Suggs

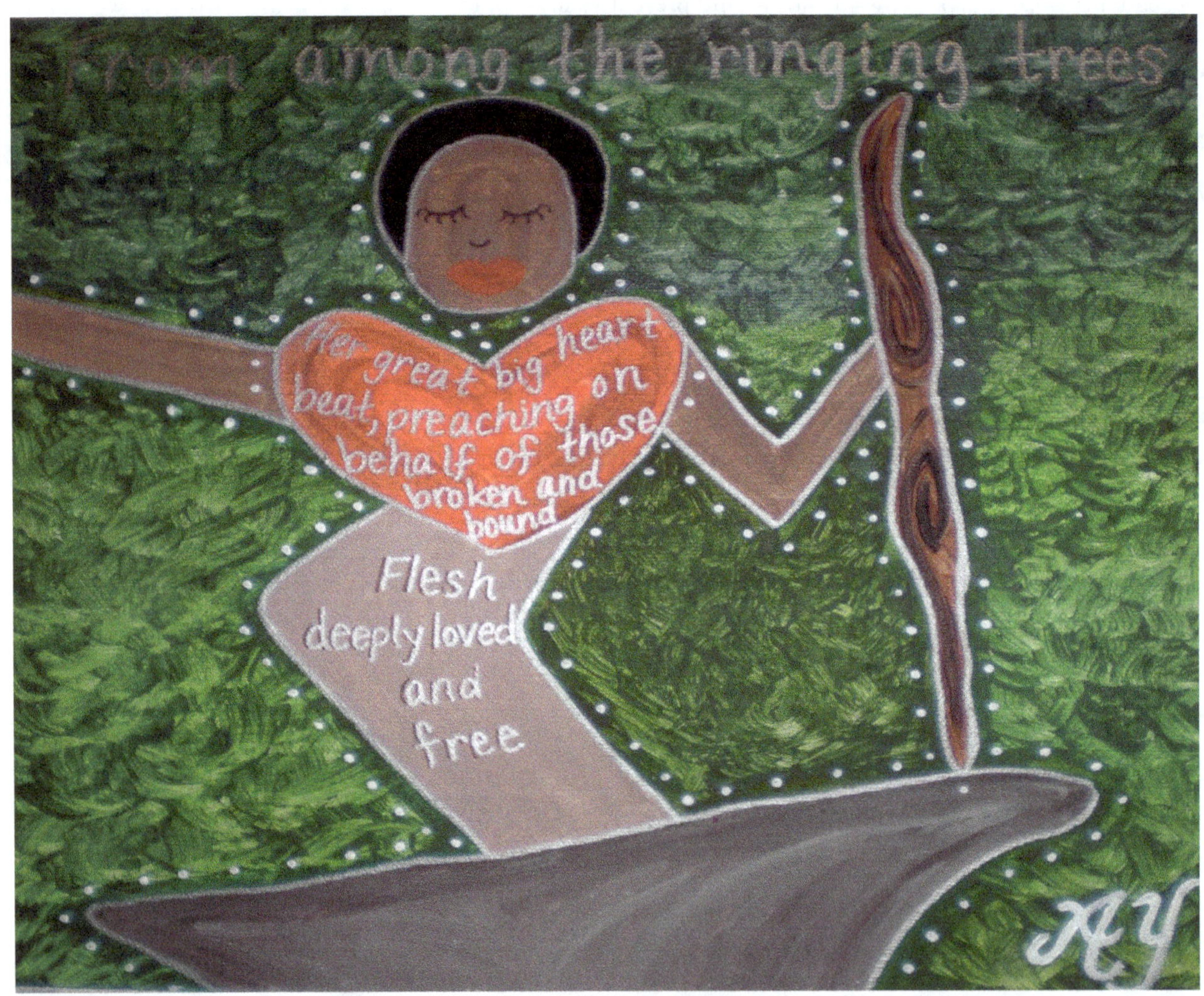

Baby Suggs
Acrylic on Canvas, 12x12

Baby Suggs

I'd like to focus on a holy woman whose preaching embodied eschatological imagination and whose dance liberated broken bodies. This holy woman cannot be found within the confines of scripture or met in the flesh. Rather, her preaching and dancing are bound within the pages of Toni Morrison's novel, *Beloved.* If ever there was a holy woman who preached on behalf of all those broken and bound it was Morrison's stunning character, Baby Suggs, holy.

Eschatological imagination is a communal foretaste of resurrection that does not suppress the social conflicts and injustices of racism, poverty, slavery, and privilege. Through the preaching and dancing of Baby Suggs, enslaved bodies are redeemed and transformed into resurrected bodies. A slave herself, Baby Suggs leads all the black men, women, and children to a clearing each week for worship. After inviting men to dance, children to laugh, and women to cry, she offers up one of the most beautiful sermons on behalf of her enslaved community. Morrison describes the efficacy of Baby Suggs' message, saying:

"She did not tell them to clean up their lives or to go and sin no more. She did not tell them they were blessed of the earth, its inheriting meek or its glory-bound pure. She told them the only grace they could have was the grace they could imagine. That if they could not see it, they would not have it." (Toni Morrison, *Beloved,* 1987, 88-89.)

Rather than proclaiming that we'll "understand it better by and by," Baby Suggs invokes heaven-on-earth in the here-and-now. In a manner similar to the many double entendres embedded in early spirituals—where the message of liberation is encoded in the message of salvation—this old black slave woman uses her voice and body to assert the freedom of eschatological imagination, proclaiming:

> *"Here," she said, "in this here place, we flesh; flesh that weeps, laughs, flesh that dances on bare feet in grass. Love it. Love it hard. Yonder they do not love your flesh. They despise it. They don't love your eyes; they'd just as soon pick 'em out. No more do they love the skin on your back. Yonder they flay it. And O my people they do not love your hands. They only use, tie, bind, chop off and leave empty. Love your hands! Love them. Raise them up and kiss them. Touch others with them, pat them together, stroke them on your face 'cause they don't love that either. You got to love it, you! And no, they ain't in love with your mouth. Yonder, out there, they will see it broken and break it again. What you say out of it they will not heed. What you scream from it they do not hear. What you put into it to nourish your body they will snatch away and give you leavins instead. No, they don't love your mouth. You got to love it.*
>
> *This is flesh I'm talking about here. Flesh that needs to be loved. Feet that need to rest and to dance; backs that need support; shoulders that need arms, strong arms I'm telling you. And O my people, out yonder, hear me, they do not love your neck unnoosed and straight. So love your neck; put a hand on it, grace it, stroke it and hold it up. And all your inside parts that they'd just as soon slop for hogs, you got to love them. The dark, dark liver—love it, love it, and the beat and beating heart, love that too. More than eyes or feet. More than lungs that have yet to draw free air. More than your life-holding womb and your life-giving private parts, hear me now, love your heart. For this is the prize."*

> *Saying no more, she stood up then and danced with her twisted hip the rest of what her heart had to say while the others opened their mouths and gave her the music. Long notes held until the four-part harmony was perfect enough for their deeply loved flesh.* (Toni Morrison, *Beloved,* 1987, 88-89.)

Resembling the ring shout typified in the brush/hush harbors of slave worship, Baby Suggs dances in response to the redemption her broken body feels and experiences. And her community of faith—those gathered in the clearing—respond with their own dances. Their dances and words may not end suffering, but they make life more livable. Such dance, proclamation, and the underlying concept of eschatological imagination are the inspirations behind my icon of Baby Suggs. Situated on a large, flat-sided rock she stands erect and proud, even with her twisted hip. From the squared canvas she proclaims the Word:

From among the ringing trees
Her great, big heart beat,
Preaching on behalf of all those broken and bound
Flesh deeply loved and free

And it is because of the proclamation of strong women like Baby Suggs that the bodies of black women and men find liberation, their dances pulling the very pieces of heaven down to earth so that all may find freedom and equality here and now. Or, as womanist activist and author, Alice Walker, once stated so poignantly, "No one can end suffering except through dance."

Questions for Contemplation:
Turning Inward:
How might you better love your flesh?
Turning Outward:
How can you work toward creating a world where the flesh of persons of color are honored and valued?

Fatima

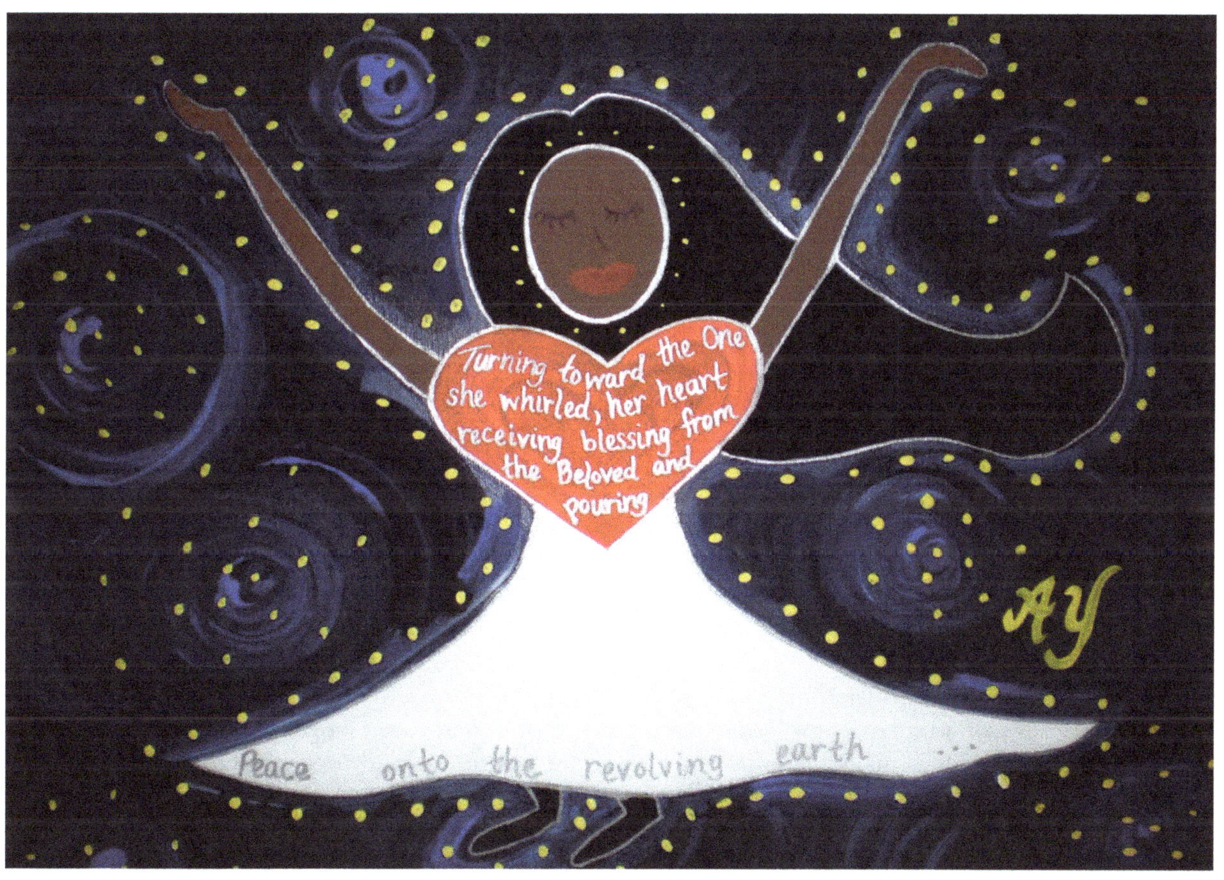

Fatima
Acrylic on Canvas, 16x20

Fatima

She performs ablutions, prays, and mends shoes for years only to don her death shroud upon her back and place a symbolic tombstone upon her head. With death cloaking her compassionate body, she begins to twirl, invoking the name of the Beloved within her heart. She is a whirling dervish and her name is Fatima. The daughter-in-law of the esteemed Sufi poet, Rumi, joins with the myriad other Holy Women Icons.

Fatima is best understood when placed in an historical context. So, I begin with a very brief history of the whirling dervishes, while also offering glimpses into women's roles in the Mevlevi Order. The primary Islamic sect that proclaims that dancing is a way of connecting with the divine—for both men and women—is the Sufi Order. Over eight hundred years ago, Mevlâna Jalâluddîn Rumi inspired faithful Muslims to whirl in harmony with all things in nature. The whirling dervishes of Turkey unite the mind, heart, and body, and help to usher peace into the world through their dance by dedicating their lives to service and compassion. After Rumi's death on December 17, 1273, his followers responded by whirling. These followers of Rumi are known as the Mevlevi Order, or more popularly, the whirling dervishes. Until around the fourteenth century women were included in the practice and leadership of turning. As Muslims in Turkey became more and more conservative, however, women were forced to the sidelines and not allowed to whirl. And even with the secularization of the country with the reign of Mustafa Kemal Ataturk, women were still denied access to the turning path because Ataturk essentially made whirling illegal in an attempt to take away as much religion from Turkish life as possible. Ataturk banned *tekkes*, or dervish homes, in 1925 as he secularized the state. By the 1970s the Turkish government allowed turning once again, but only if it was a performance and not a prayer. There were even reports of an old dervish being arrested because they saw his lips mouthing "Allah" as he turned in a theatre performance for tourists.

In the West, however, the Mevlevi Order of America was formed and women were again permitted in the turning path. Every December 17 a myriad of whirling women gather for *sema*, remembering Rumi's union with the Beloved, and turning in solidarity with the earth.

Before Western women began to whirl, however, women found inclusion and affirmation in the Mevlevi Order in Turkey. The inclusion of women in the early developments of turning was based primarily on the women in relationship with Rumi, such as his daughter-in-law, Fatima. Further, his granddaughters, Seref and Mutahhara were pivotal in helping their brother, Ulu Arif Chelebi, develop the Mevlevi Order. Additionally, Arifa Hoslika, a follower of Rumi, by the time Sultan Veled was made *Pir* of the Order and was initiated as a *halife* by Ulu Arif. A *halife* is usually the *sheikh's* successor or the primary representative of the Order in the world; for a woman to be given such an honor speaks to the primacy of empowering women in the early phases of the Mevlevi Order. In the same way, women were initiated as *postneshins*, or the one who leads the turning ritual, and women were also deemed successors to be the *sheikha*, or leader, of the *tekke*. For a woman to lead the covenant of communal life designed to accommodate the dervish lifestyle, also known as the *tekke*, is a highest honor and responsibility.

Selaheddin Zarkub increased the number of women devoted to Rumi's teachings. Zarkub's daughters, Fatima and Hediyya, and his wife, Latifa, learned about Sufism through Rumi's teachings. He taught them to read the Qur'an and referred to Fatima as his "right eye" and Hediyya his "left eye" and Latifa "the personification of God's grace." One of Rumi's greatest joys was when Fatima married his son Sultan Veled. Fatima developed as a mystic under Rumi's tutelage and Sultan Veled eventually became Rumi's successor to the evolving order.

This is only a brief glimpse into Fatima's fascinating history and the birth of the whirling dervishes. If you are interested in learning more about this topic, I detail it further in my book, *Embodying the Feminine in the Dances of the World's Religions*, as does Shakina Reinhertz in *Women Called to the Path of Rumi: The Way of the Whirling Dervish.*

It is clear that this whirling mystic, Fatima, was an important part of the Sufi path. Cloaked in the same clothing as men, turning on the same polished floor, she whirled, her heart crying out to us:

Turning toward the One she whirled,
her heart receiving blessing from the Beloved and pouring peace onto the revolving earth…

Fatima's dancing body—as portrayed in the icon—exemplifies the symbolic movement vocabulary essential to whirling. Her right palm faces up so as to receive blessings from the Beloved. Her body is then a conduit for that divine grace and blessing. As the love of Allah courses through her body, it exits out her left hand as her palm faces down toward the earth, bestowing blessings and peace as she revolves. Her dancing body stands as a paradigm for all the women who have whirled in union with the Beloved. May Fatima's whirling body inspire our bodies to become conduits for grace and peace, bestowing blessings upon the whole earth with open hands.

Questions for Contemplation:
Turning Inward:
How can you better connect to the Beloved that dwells within your heart?
Turning Outward:
How can you use your open hands to bestow blessings upon the earth and all humanity?

Frida Kahlo

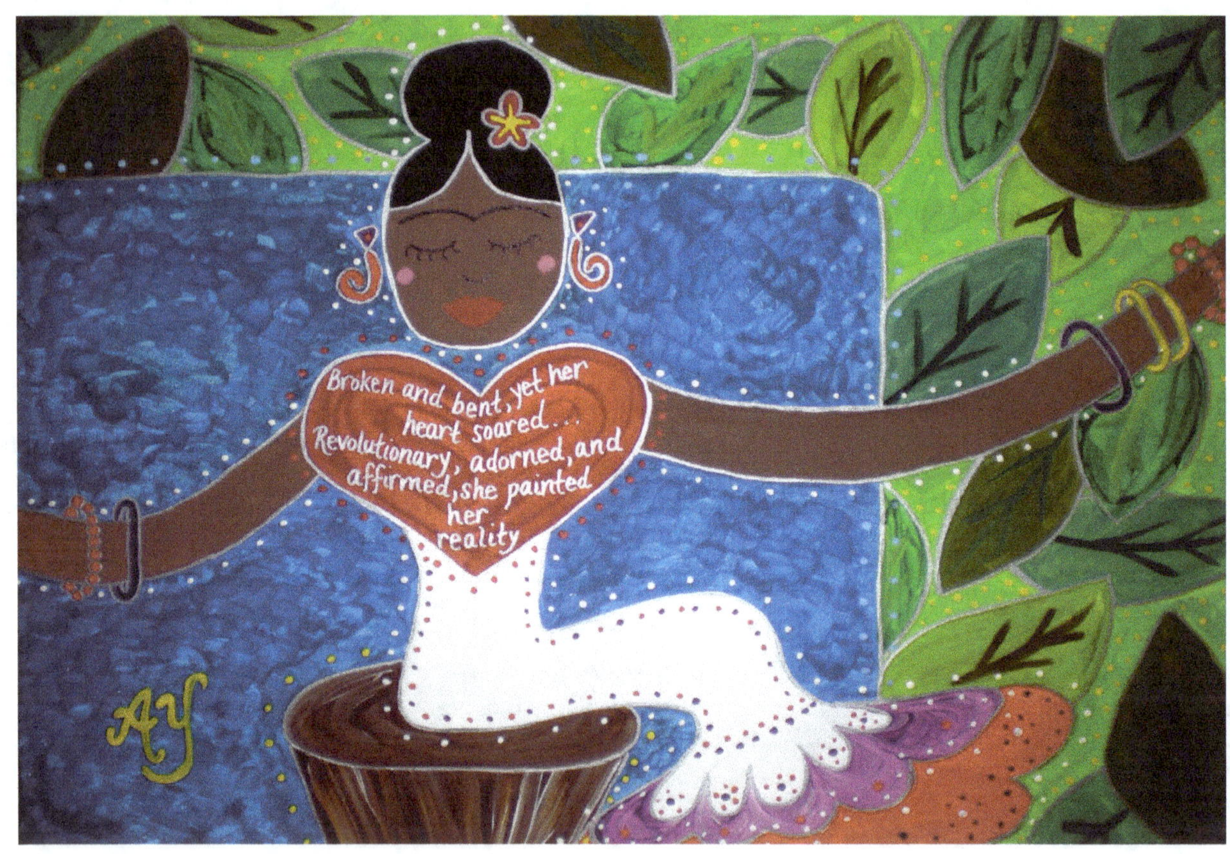

Frida Kahlo
Acrylic on Canvas, 16x20

Friday Kahlo

Ever the revolutionary, Frida Kahlo insisted that she was born on July 7, 1910, which is three years and one day *later* than her birth certificate indicates. Believing so deeply in the Mexican Revolution, Kahlo wanted her life to begin with the modern life of Mexico. During adolescence she never showed a tremendous interest in art. But in September of 1925 everything changed. Kahlo was injured while riding a bus that collided with a trolley in Mexico City. An iron handrail pierced her abdomen and uterus, thus making difficult her ability to conceive. Covered in the gold dust of another passenger on board, she was rushed to the hospital only to discover that she had a broken spinal column, collarbone, ribs, and pelvis, along with eleven fractures in her right leg, a dislocated shoulder, and a crushed and dislocated right foot. It is during the subsequent three months in a full body cast that Kahlo began experimenting with painting in earnest.

It wasn't long before Frida Kahlo and the famous Mexican muralist, Diego Rivera, fell in love. Over time, they became part of the "spiritual landscape of Mexico, like Popocatepeti and Iztaccihuatl in the valley of Anahuac (Hayden Herrera, *Frida*, 106)." Though she savored her role as the adoring and beautiful wife of the genius artist, she was also a feminist, artist, and political revolutionary in her own right. In fact, one may say that Frida Kahlo was the inaugurator of folk feminist art, emblematic of national and indigenous traditions, offering an unwavering depiction of the female form and experience. Upon marrying Rivera, she maintained her own last name, something almost unheard of in 1929. This gesture was indicative of her stance on many issues.

Their marriage was a troubled one. Though he was never esteemed as particularly handsome, Rivera was charming and was a well-known lady's man. No doubt, he was unfaithful, including a marriage-ending tryst with Kahlo's younger sister, Cristina. The couple remarried one year after being divorced. Frida, a sexually fluid woman, also cheated on Diego. Most famous among her affairs were artist Isamu Noguchi and dancer/singer/actress Josephine Baker. Like her husband, Kahlo did not feel confined to the boundaries society placed upon married couples, artists, or women in general.

Kahlo is remembered for saying, "I suffered two grave accidents in my life. One in which a streetcar knocked me down…The other accident is Diego." Her life was riddled with anguish. She suffered physically from her bus accident; she suffered emotionally from her intense love and utter despair enmeshed in her marriage; and she suffered spiritually as a Mexican revolutionary who longed for equal treatment for all her people. This suffering, of course, manifested itself in her painting, both on canvas and on her body. In her countless self portraits we gaze at one who adorned her body with the classic Mexican dress, which she claimed "has been created by the people for the people." Ribbons, ruffles, bright colors, jewels, and sashes increased as Kahlo's health decreased. Herrara claims that "Frida's decoration was touching: it was at once an affirmation of her love of life and a signal of her awareness—and defiance—of pain and death (Hererra, *Frida*, 113)."

As I considered how I might pay homage to this revolutionary feminist artist, I knew at once she must be seated in front of casa azul, the home that birthed her love of painting, the home where she first learned of revolution, the home where she thrived most, and the home where she suffered most. Draped in the dress that connected her more fully with her people and the earth, Frida gazes back at us, her arms outstretched in a gesture of embrace, as though she is liberating the Mexican people she loved so deeply. Seated in front of the home where she learned to paint her reality, her heart speaks to us:

Broken and bent
Yet her heart soared…
Revolutionary, adorned
And affirmed,
She painted her reality

Kahlo's reality was one of suffering—individually and corporately. In these ways she emboldens us to power on, creating beauty in the midst of suffering, and seeking to create a world where all humanity is treated equally.

Questions for Contemplation:
Turning Inward:
Has there been a time in your life when your suffering brought about revelation and beauty?
Turning Outward:
What can you do to be a revolutionary who inspires the marginalized?

Mary

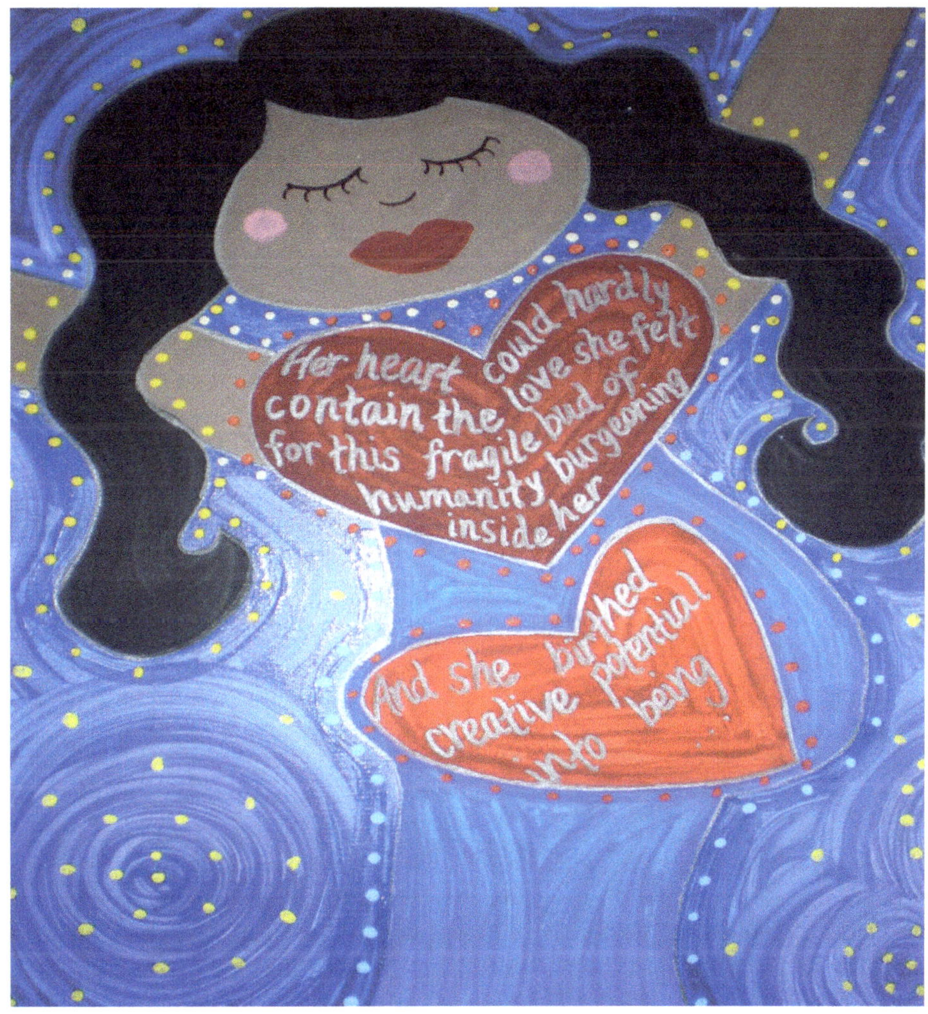

Mary
Acrylic on Canvas, 16x20, Arce Private Collection

Mary

Many feminists struggle with the Virgin Mary, insisting that she is often used to illustrate the submissive role of women in the church. Still others adhere to essentialist understandings of her stories, claiming liberation from some kind of inborn and innate feminine power. In these ways, some feminists highlight the story of Mary as an example of the divine feminine nature of God, gestating in the womb and birthing the sacred into being. This is a powerful way of talking about divine incarnation, of God enfleshing Godself into earthly reality through the expanding womb of young Mary.

Along these lines, Marcia Mount Shoop expounds upon Jesus' birth in her book about embodiment and the body of Christ called *Let the Bones Dance*. She writes:

Has anybody ever thought about Mary having contractions?
Yes, she had contractions.
But there is just that one line, something like…
"and then the time came that she would be delivered" or whatever.
She had Jesus in a barn, for Christ's sake.
She had to let out at least a few shrieks along the way.

Has anybody ever acknowledged that Mary had a cervix,
much less that it dilated and was all stretched and bloody?
What was it like for her?
What was it like for her?
Breathing, sweating,
gripping whatever was closest to her determined hand…
What was it like to labor with God that way?
(Shoop, 72-73)

And these words have power, power of overcoming our Docetic desires that sterilize Jesus' birth, that wipe away the manure in the manger, and instead birth a squeaky clean Christ into a Renaissance painting where Mary's porcelain flesh shimmers under her blue embroidered Shakespearean gown as she holds a white baby Jesus whose golden hair matches the halo around his clean head. We don't really want to think about the holy's cervix. But it's there, dilated and pushing, groaning the light of love into the world.

Meister Eckhart says, "For all eternity, God lies on a birthing bed, giving birth. The essence of God is Birthing." But these claims are also problematic because, while it's sometimes difficult to speak of Mary's cervix, it's easy to essentialize what it means to be woman and to equate women's holiness with their capacity to give birth. As we feminists struggle to elevate Mary's spiritual status, we sometimes forget that speaking of birth and gestation is not always empowering or even essential to womanhood. Advent's waiting and longing is a stark reminder to many women and men who yearn for parenthood, who desire a belly-full of divinity, who wait patiently for birth to no avail. Further, it's too easy to assume that this is the ability or desire of all women.

There are many women out there, myself included, who do not have the ability to birth children, who will never know the essence of God if the essence of God is birthing. This does not make their bodies any less worthy, any less holy. Moreover, there are many people out there who desire to be parents, but discriminatory legislation prevents them from adopting children. As my wife and I have recently welcomed a baby into our home, we are starkly aware that our state (and the state where our child was born) only allows one gay parent to adopt a child and, unless discriminatory laws change, the other one of us will never *legally* be our future child's mother. The host of implications for this discrimination are theological, for sure, but also very scary.

These notions of essentialism, feminism, birth, and discrimination are a lived reality for so many as we remember Mary's pregnancy. I painted Mary's icon, allowing her pregnancy to embolden others to birth creative potential into our world as her heart and belly proclaim:

Her heart could hardly
Contain the love she felt
For this fragile bud of humanity
Burgeoning inside her
And she birthed
Creative potential into being…

Whether it is the creative potential of new life growing in the womb, or the creative potential burgeoning inside our hearts and minds, Mary reminds us that women—and women's bodies—have the power to change the world.

Questions for Contemplation:
Turning Inward:
What creative potential is awaiting birth within you?
Turning Outward:
What steps will you take to birth this potential into being and make it a reality?

Guadalupe

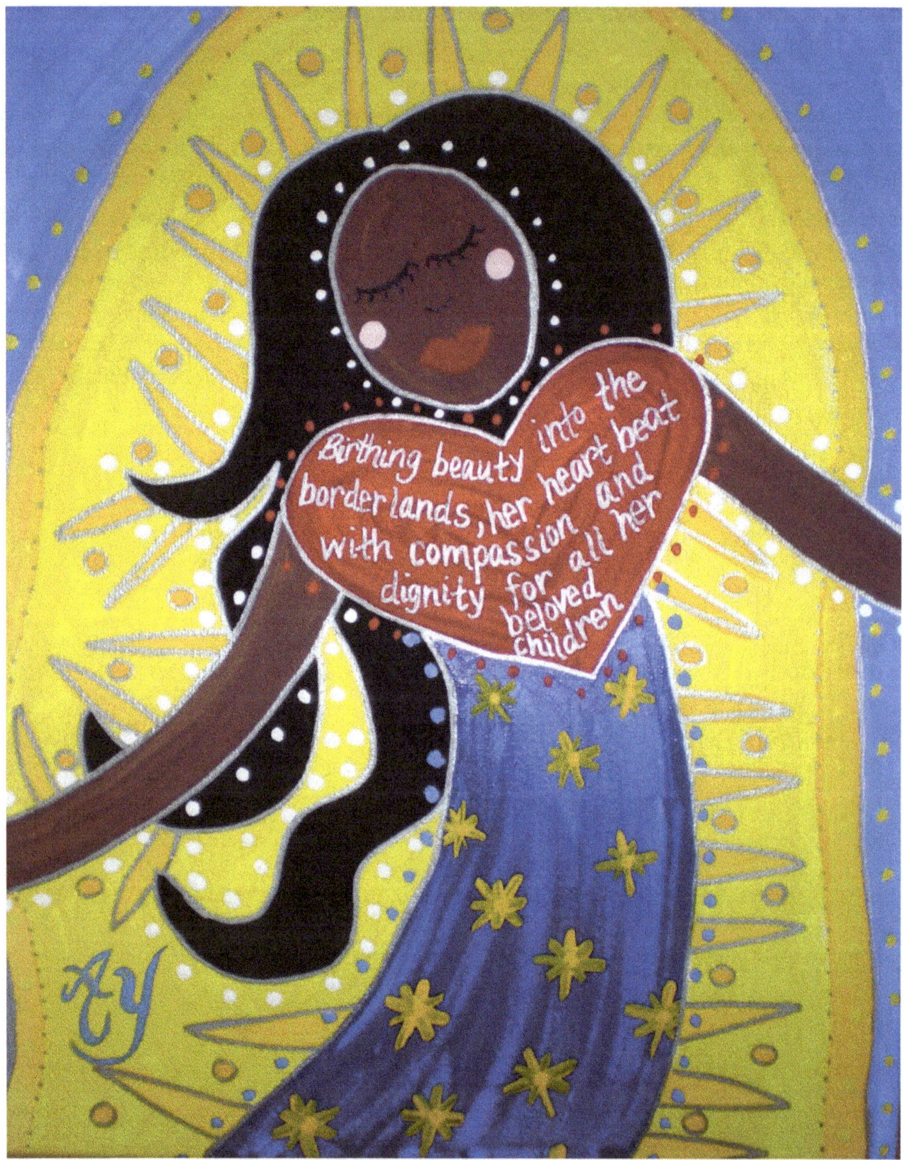

Guadalupe
Acrylic on Canvas, 11x14, Martere Private Collection

Guadalupe

It is early morning on the Hill of Tepeyak on December 9, 1531 when a wondering peasant named Juan Diego first caught a glimpse of her presence. Diego sees a vision of a teenage girl surrounded by light; the young girl asks that a church be built on the hill in her honor. After hearing her speak and seeing the light emanating from her presence, Diego recognizes her as the Virgin Mary. He rushes to the Spanish archbishop who insists on a sign as proof of Diego's vision. The young girl instructs Diego to gather flowers from the top of the hill, even though it is past their growing season. Upon climbing to the top of the Hill of Tepeyak, Diego discovers Castilian roses—a beautiful flower otherwise unheard of in Mexico—which the glowing young woman arranges in his cloak. When Diego returns to the archbishop, he opens his cloak to reveal the miraculous flowers and they fall to floor; in their place was an image imprinted on the fabric of his cloak. It was the image of Our Lady of Guadalupe.

Guadalupe is one of Mexico's most popular religious and cultural images and her icon, now on display at the Basilica of Our Lady of Guadalupe, is one of the most visited Marian shrines in the entire world. On December 12, countless Christians—particularly Catholics—celebrate her feast day. Her feast day occurs within the four week celebration of Advent, which is the period of waiting, expectancy, and gestation before the birth of Jesus at Christmas.

I was surprised when the time came for me to paint an icon in honor of Our Lady of Guadalupe. I'd intended to paint her for several years, but struggled with how to find empowerment in her traditional iconography. Then I was commissioned to paint her as a gift for an amazing young woman. A father asked me to paint Guadalupe for his daughter, a midwife who works with babies born on the border between Mexico and the United States. He shared pictures of his daughter, told me about her inspiring work, and informed me that her favorite painting of Guadalupe subverted traditional iconography by placing her in a slinky blue dress covered with shimmering stars in the foreground; in the background it is clear that she stands among prostitutes. Inspired by this midwife and her work, my painting also subverts Guadalupe's traditional image. She wears the same blue dress, but continues to be surrounded by a halo of holiness as her heart proclaims:

Birthing beauty into the borderlands,
Her heart beat with compassion and dignity
For all her beloved children.

Guadalupe emboldens us to subvert the status quo, to value the poor and marginalized, and to acknowledge the profound truth often resides at the borderlands of difference.

Questions for Contemplation:
Turning Inward:
What miracles reside in your heart and life?
Turning Outward:
How might you dwell more in the borderlands by welcoming those who are different than you?

Isadora Duncan

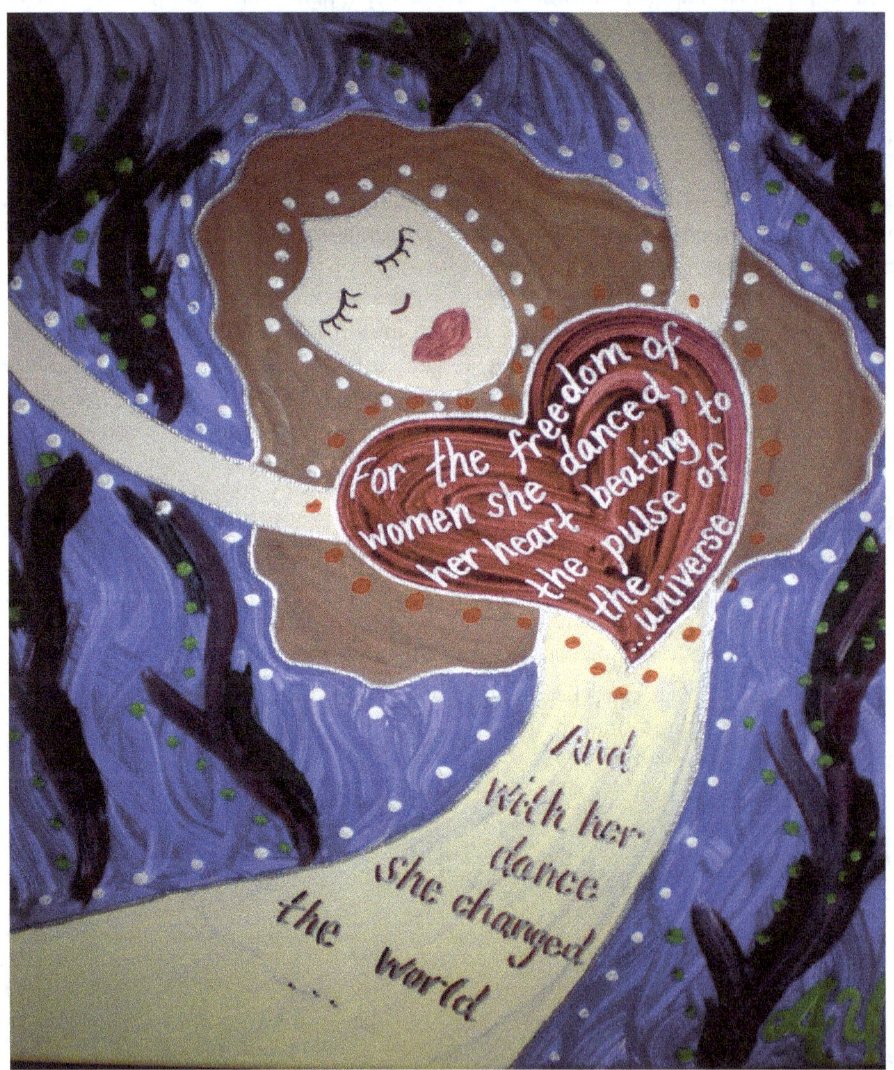

Isadora Duncan
Acrylic on Canvas, 11x14

Isadora Duncan

In May of 1877 a dancing, feminist, revolutionary was born. She was not constrained by the corsets, morals, or traditions of her time. Barefoot, clad in flowing garments, with a diaphanous scarf in hand, she stepped onto the stage and rocked the world: the world of dance, the world of women, and the world of religion.

Born in San Francisco as Dora Angela Duncan and known to us as Isadora Duncan, or Holy Isadora. This wild woman rejected the rigidity of ballet, conventional roles for women, and traditional religion. After feeling constrained by the pointe shoes, corsets, and unyielding technique of American ballet, Duncan left for Europe, intent on revolutionizing the world through dance. She claimed, "I have come to bring about a great renaissance of religion through the dance, to bring the knowledge of the beauty and holiness of the human body … (Duncan quoted by Terry Walter in *Isadora Duncan*)."

In calling for a rebirth of religion through dance, however, Duncan was not limited by the conventions of the day. Because the forms of dance capable of bringing about such a renaissance did not yet exist. It's popular and artistic forms (ballet) paralleled the attitudes toward the body ensconced in Christian values. Ballet and Christianity imposed formal moral codes: bodies as weightless, ethereal, something to overcome; toes that relevé away from the earth and toward heaven; no falls. If a dancer falls in ballet—or in traditional Christianity—it is a mistake, perhaps even a sin. In the form of modern dance Duncan created and developed, the body utilized natural and prophetic movement, focusing on the solar plexus as the center of the body, movement based on breath, contraction and release, fall and recovery, asymmetry, and organic movement found in nature.

Inspired by Greek art and statues, the movements of natural elements in the sea, wind, and trees, and her understanding of Nietzsche's revaluing of Christian values, Duncan lived without bounds. She called Nietzsche's *Thus Spoke Zarathustra* "her bible" and identified her own vision with that of Zarathustra. She believed that her dance would help women overcome their faith in an otherworldly God by educating them to an awareness of their own bodily being as holy and beautiful, as the source of their highest ideals. Kimerer LaMothe thoughtfully recounts Duncan's use of Nietzsche in her book *Nietzsche's Dancers*. Idealizing the philosopher who claimed he could only believe in a God who could dance, Duncan states, "If my art is symbolic for any one thing, it is symbolic of the freedom of woman and her emancipation from the hide-bound conventions that are the warp and woof of Puritanism (*Isadora Speaks*, 44)."

Freeing women, revolutionizing religion, and developing an entirely new dance form paralleled the unconventionality of Duncan's personal life. In both facets—personal and professional—Duncan dismantled stereotypes. She birthed two children out of wedlock with two different men, and after her children tragically died in a car accident, it is rumored that she had an affair with a woman. Like her dance and her philosophy, her sexuality was also fluid and unconstrained by the mores of her time. And for this fluidity—in life, in dance, in morals, in religion—she was highly criticized. Her bare feet, flowing dresses, and sometimes bare breasts were dubbed scandalous. At times, she was called a fraud, her dance considered by some critics to be nothing more than rolling on the ground, waving a scarf, and grasping the air. Amidst the controversies of her dance, her religion, and her love life, Duncan believed that "every artist worth anything has always been vilified. It is the price the world demands for the beauty we invoke (*Isadora Speaks*, 50)."

Ultimately, tragedy reigned supreme in Duncan's life as her children were killed, her lover committed suicide, and drunkenness and poverty consumed her later years. And it is ironic that her fluidity—the very virtue that set women free, revolutionized dance, and revalued religion—is what led to her death. In an act of glamour, the dancing diva thrust the silk scarf around her neck out a car window so that it would billow in the wind; the scarf got tangled in the wheel and strangled her.

Amidst her fits of passion and drunken rages, Duncan remains holy still, worthy to join my other Holy Women Icons. Why? Why should I deem this seemingly wanton woman "holy"?

As a professional dancer whose toes have bled through my pointe shoes and whose body wasted away in ballet classes, I think of Duncan each time my bare and unbound feet step onto the dance floor. Modern dance set me free. As a lesbian who thought for so many years that marrying a man would be the only way I could be ordained, acceptable, holy, valid, I think of Duncan each Sunday when I step into the pulpit. Fluid sexuality set me free. As a queer feminist scholar of religion who seeks to reject, deconstruct, and revalue what has been used to oppress, marginalize, and violate, I think of Duncan when I read Nietzsche, scripture, theology. Her approach to religion set me free.

So, it was no surprise that, with bare feet and an open heart, I painted a canvas filled with the flow of nature. A dancing woman stands center stage, her arms outstretched in natural, free, and unbound movement, as her heart cries out to us:

For the freedom of women she danced,
Her heart beating to the pulse of the universe…
And with her dance
She changed the world…

She changed the world of dance. She changed the world of religion. She changed the world of women. For these things, we will never forget Holy Isadora.

Questions for Contemplation:
Turning Inward:
How can you unbind and free your own body?
Turning Outward:
What steps can you take to make more women celebrate their bodies as holy and beloved?

Jarena Lee

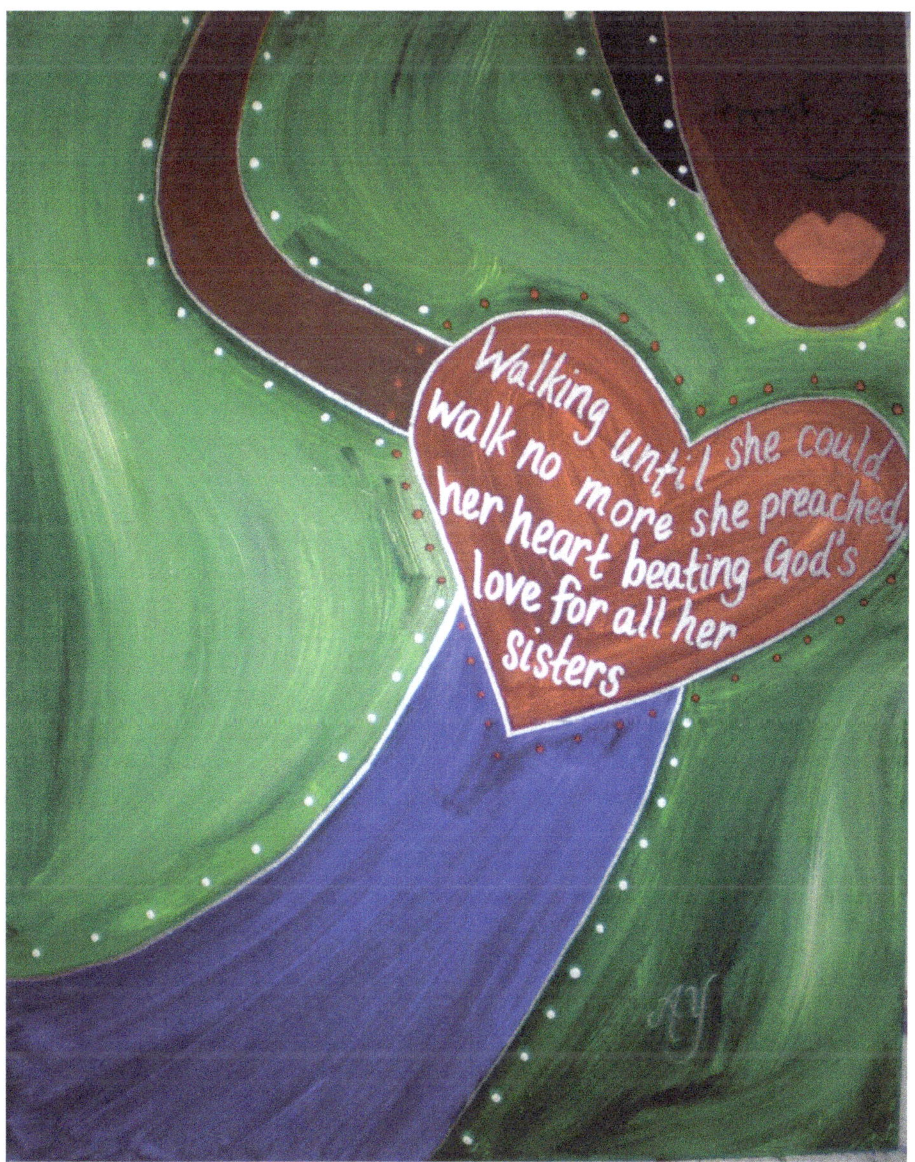

Jarena Lee
Acrylic on Canvas, 16x20

Jarena Lee

Around the time I published my second book, *The Gendered Pulpit: Sex, Body, and Desire in Preaching and Worship*, I started thinking a lot about women preachers, adding more to my collection of Holy Women Icons. As I celebrate the privilege I have as queer feminist to stand behind the pulpit each Sunday—to gender the space in the direction of justice—I must also recall the myriad holy women who have gone before me. I think specifically of my sister preachers, those who raised their voices in bold proclamations when the road was long and unimaginably difficult. I think of preachers like Jarena Lee.

Lee spent thirty years as an itinerant preacher and was the first black woman to be licensed to preach through the African Methodist Episcopal (AME) church. Despite the fact that the AME issued a definitive ruling that women were *not* permitted to preach in 1852, Lee spent the bulk of her adult life preaching. Jarena Lee's struggle to preach is a familiar story in nineteenth-century American Protestantism, even though the Second Awakening ushered in a period of intense religious revival; with camp meetings around every corner, there was an unprecedented opportunity for women to preach. Like Jarena Lee, though, they weren't paid, ordained, or protected.

Lee moved from New Jersey to Philadelphia when she was 21 and told the famous Richard Allen that she was called by the Spirit to preach. Since the AME's book of discipline didn't say anything about women preachers yet, Allen asked her to hold off for a bit. So, she did what many frustrated women called to preach did; she married a preacher. Six years into the marriage her husband died and she knew she could no longer ignore her calling.

So, Jarena Lee left her two children in the care of people at church and hit the road. Her journals indicate that in one year alone she walked 2,325 miles and preached 178 sermons; that's more than three sermons per week and six miles per day. And before we pass judgment on Lee for leaving her children in the care of others, it's important to acknowledge her context in order to understand the power of her journey. According to homiletics scholar Anna Carter Florence:

> Preaching is a way of living and speaking in right relationship with God. It is a way of standing in one's own life, before God and others. A preacher who denies this denies her very self; she goes down into the pit. She gets swallowed by the whale. She gets tossed this way and that until she relinquishes false notions of what her life should be and submits to God. And God does not adhere to human articulations of polity: God calls whom God will. If the preacher is a poor black woman in antebellum Philadelphia in the year 1811, a woman whom no one will believe and for whom living out the call will be unimaginably difficult, so be it: God does not call preachers to *be believed.* God calls preachers to *preach.* Lee had tried standing in someone else's life; it hadn't worked. She was ready to stand on her own. (Florence, *Preaching as Testimony*, 44)

So, standing on her own two feet, sanctified and called, the Spirit led Jarena Lee into the thirty years of wilderness preaching alone. She received no salary. She was dependent on charity and kindness for shelter and food. "Certain poverty, strenuous travel, broken health, exhausting pace: these were the rigors that defined iterant life, and for thirty years, Lee lived with them (Florence, 45)." Abiding in that broken wilderness is what made Jarena Lee both holy and human. Broken and flourishing.

When I think of women who have gendered the pulpit in the direction of justice, I think of Jerena Lee. Evoking a sense of movement, as though she is walking right off the canvas, and surrounded by shades of green that covered the trails she walked from pulpit to pulpit, Lee's heart proclaims the Word:

Walking until she could walk no more,
She preached,
Her heart beating God's love
For all her sisters.

When our feet grow weary and our voices shake, when gendering the pulpit overwhelms us and we fear we cannot go on, let us remember the mighty proclamations of Jarena Lee. When we gender the pulpit in the direction of justice, we ordain her spirit with gratitude for the many miles she walked and the countless sermons she preached. Thank you, Jarena Lee, for raising your voice. Let us now raise our voices.

Questions for Contemplation:
Turning Inward:
What are you called to do?
Turning Outward:
What is holding you back from pursuing your calling?

Mary Daly

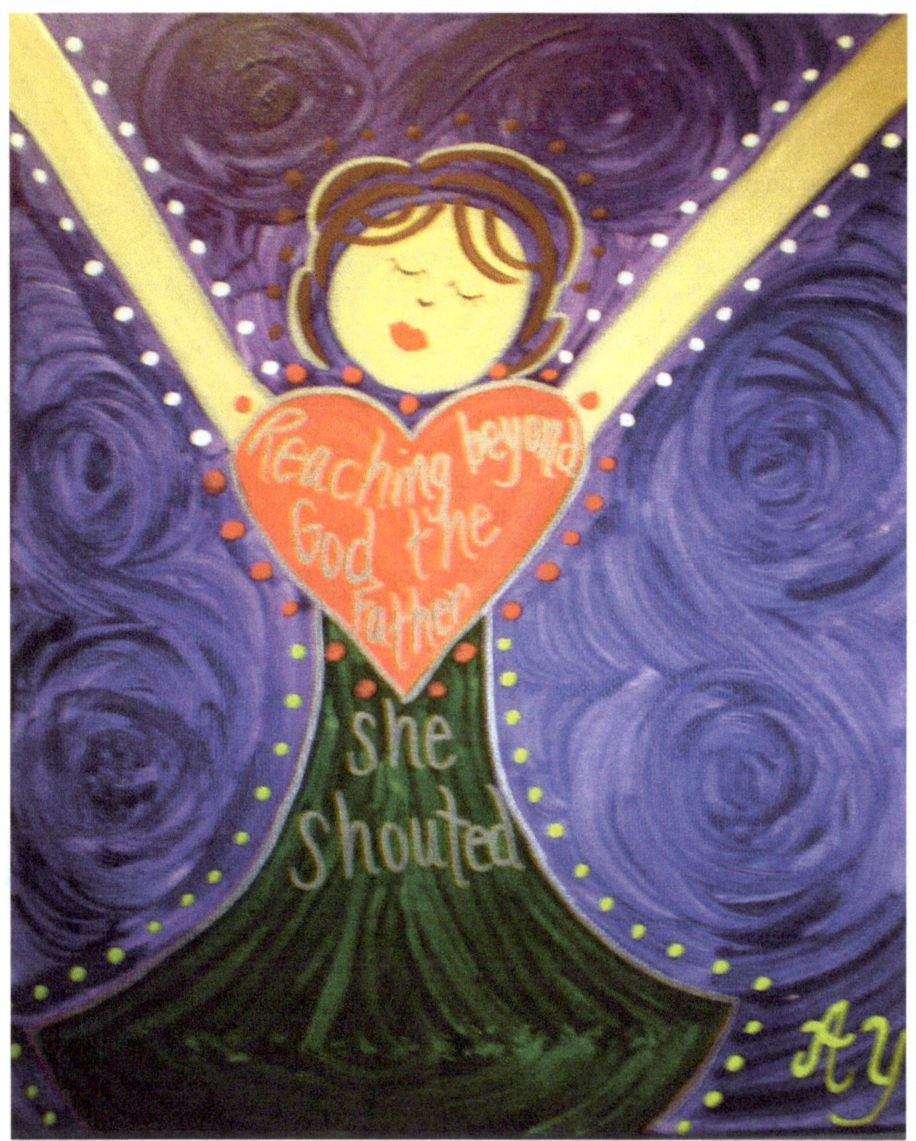

Mary Daly
Acrylic on Canvas, 11x14

Mary Daly

You don't have to be perfect to be a saint. The saints who comprise my Holy Women Icons are far from perfect, but each one has made a difference in the lives of countless women. By giving iconography a folk feminist twist—by painting these women and calling them holy—it is my hope that their lives can embolden us to stand for justice, equality, and peace in the ways they did.

Mary Daly (1928-2010) described herself as a "radical lesbian feminist." She was a philosopher, theologian, and writer who taught at Boston College, a Jesuit-run institution, for 33 years. Controversy erupted in1999 when Daly either retired or was forced to leave (there is debate about which is most accurate) after violating university policy by refusing to allow male students in her advanced women's studies courses. But Daly was no stranger to controversy as she dedicated her life to women's rights, overturning patriarchy, subverting oppressive religious traditions, and writing eight books along the way.

For many women, reading Mary Daly's pivotal *The Church and the Second Sex* or *Beyond God the Father* were their first forays into feminist theology. As in my icon, Daly stands left of center. Some would say she stands so far left that she dangles off the spectrum altogether. But we cannot forget Daly's time and context: teaching and receiving tenure when there were no other women in her department, writing and researching about feminist theology, a field that many academics didn't even think existed.

Daly has been critiqued for being an essentialist, for ignoring the voices of women of color, and even for being transphobic. These critiques—often justified—weighed heavy on my mind and heart as I contemplated canonizing her as a Holy Woman Icon. By painting her icon, would I be condoning all that she did in her lifetime? By calling her holy, was I excusing everything she ever said that was unfair or unjust? These questions plagued me as I considered painting an icon of Daly.

When she passed away on January 3, 2010 I was surprised at my emotional response. There were still elements of her work that troubled me. I continued to feel that many of the critiques raised against her by other feminist, womanist, mujerista, and queer theologians were valid. But with her death I also felt a loss. The feminist community had lost a forerunner. Feminist theologians—whether we agree with all that she said and did during her lifetime—are indebted to the groundwork Mary Daly laid. When I was a young woman in college grappling with my calling as a minister, scholar, and artist, I remember reading Mary Daly's work. I remember feeling as though *Beyond God the Father* was written like she was shouting, angry, outraged at the way the church, patriarchy, and religion have treated women. I, too, was angry. I was angry that the only God I'd ever learned about was a father, a male. Reading Daly's writing was my first step toward moving beyond that kind of God. Her work helped teach me that sometimes there is a need to shout.

These formative feminist memories combined with my memories of my first personal encounter with Mary Daly as I spread my canvas to paint her icon. I remembered attending the American Academy of Religion in Philadelphia in

2005. I went to a session on feminism and religion and Mary Daly was on the program. I was there early, studious with a pen in hand, eager to learn. Daly walked in wearing green sweatpants and what looked like house slippers; she took one look at the table for panelists and the rows of chairs and scoffed. She announced that she and the panel wouldn't use the table and we would put all the chairs in a circle for a more egalitarian discussion. It was both hilarious and meaningful at the same time.

So, there was no doubt that Daly's icon would be wearing green, her arms outstretched because her body was worth the space it occupied in the world. Most of my icons include a heart as the entire torso of the holy women; the heart speaks a series of words on the canvas. As I painted and remembered Mary Daly's life, it was clear what her heart would say:

Reaching beyond God the Father
She shouted

For women who have always been told to keep quiet, Mary Daly raised her voice. Because of that, we are empowered to do the same. For this, Mary Daly becomes holy. Not perfect. Not without fault. But holy.

Questions for Contemplation:
Turning Inward:
What inside of you must be released in a hearty shout?
Turning Outward:
How can you raise your voice so that other women can be empowered to shout, as well?

Pachamama

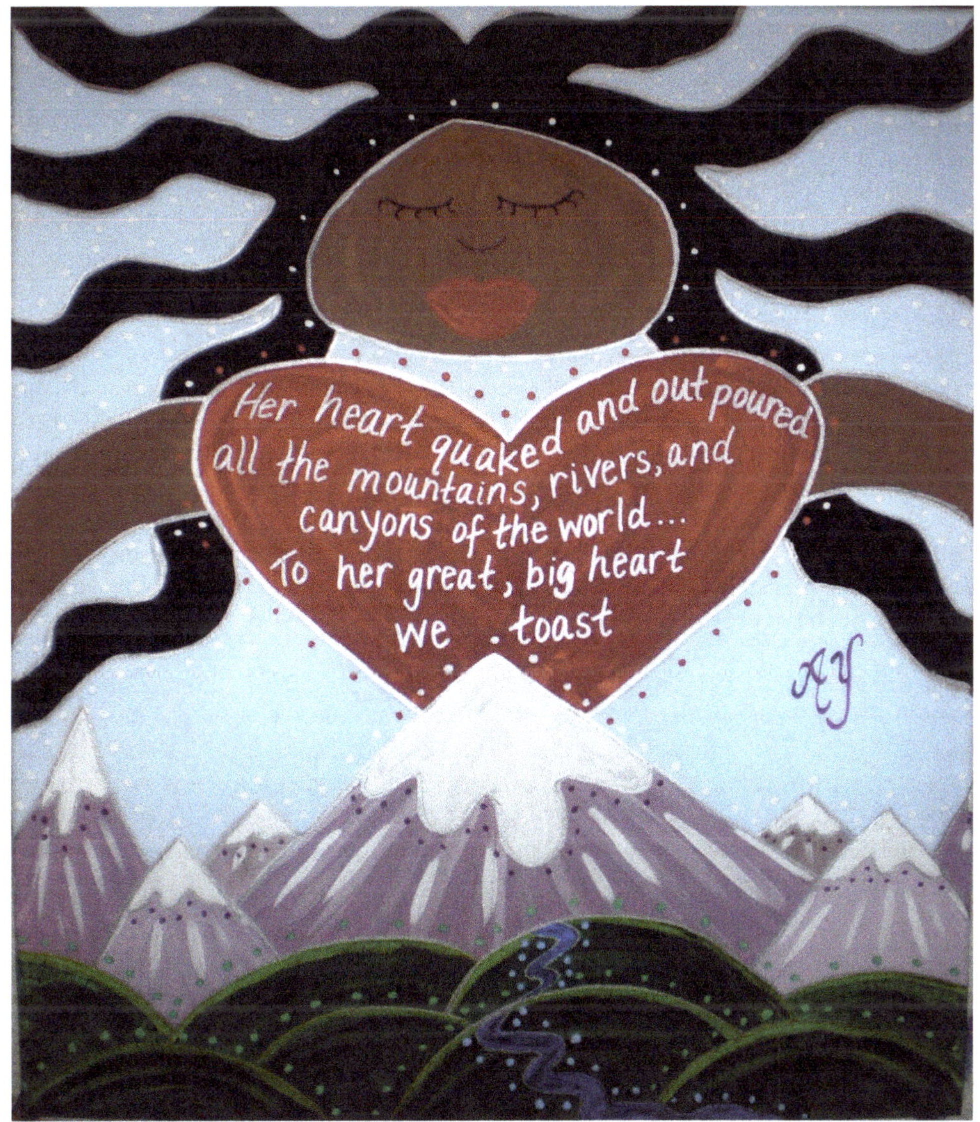

Pachamama
Acrylic on Canvas, 16x20

Pachamama

The indigenous people of the Andes celebrate a high holy season in Incan mythology each August, honoring their beloved Pachamama. Pachamama is venerated as the earth goddess and during August, her followers give her payment (*pago*) with their central ritual of *Challa.*

Pachamama translates more literally as "mother world" and she is the fertility goddess who presides over planting, farming, and harvesting. In these ways, she is quite benevolent, but she can also become angry and cause earthquakes. Because of her association with fertility and nature, people often pour a small amount of *chicha* or wine into the dirt before drinking, as a way of expressing gratitude to Pachamama for the bounty of the earth. The spilling of drink onto the ground becomes a holy offering. Similarly, her followers often raise a toast to her before festivals, meals, or upon traveling through the Andes. This toast is daily called *challa*, which is also the name of the festival in her honor throughout the month of August.

Pachamama is said to be married to Inti, but with the convergence of Catholicism in Peru she has become more of a Virgin Mary figure for many converts. At worst, this is a classic example of indigenous traditions being "baptized" or altered to fit the desires of colonialists. At best, it is an example of the strength of Andean women to maintain their heritage and beliefs during the onslaught of western missionaries.

Either way, Pachamama prevails. Her body is one with the Andes and she births the caverns, canyons, and rivers that sustain the earth. So, every August, I raise my glass to Pachamama, toasting her bounteous spirit as her icon gazes back at all her followers, her heart proclaiming:

Her heart quaked and out poured
All the mountains, rivers, and canyons of the world…
To her great, big heart
We toast

With our Andean sisters and the souls of Peru, let us remember this earth goddess each time we raise our glasses to toast what is good, beautiful, and holy.

Questions for Contemplation:
Turning Inward:
What parts of the earth are you most grateful?
Turning Outward:
How can you better express you gratitude to Pachamama and the earth for its beauty and bounty?

Gaia

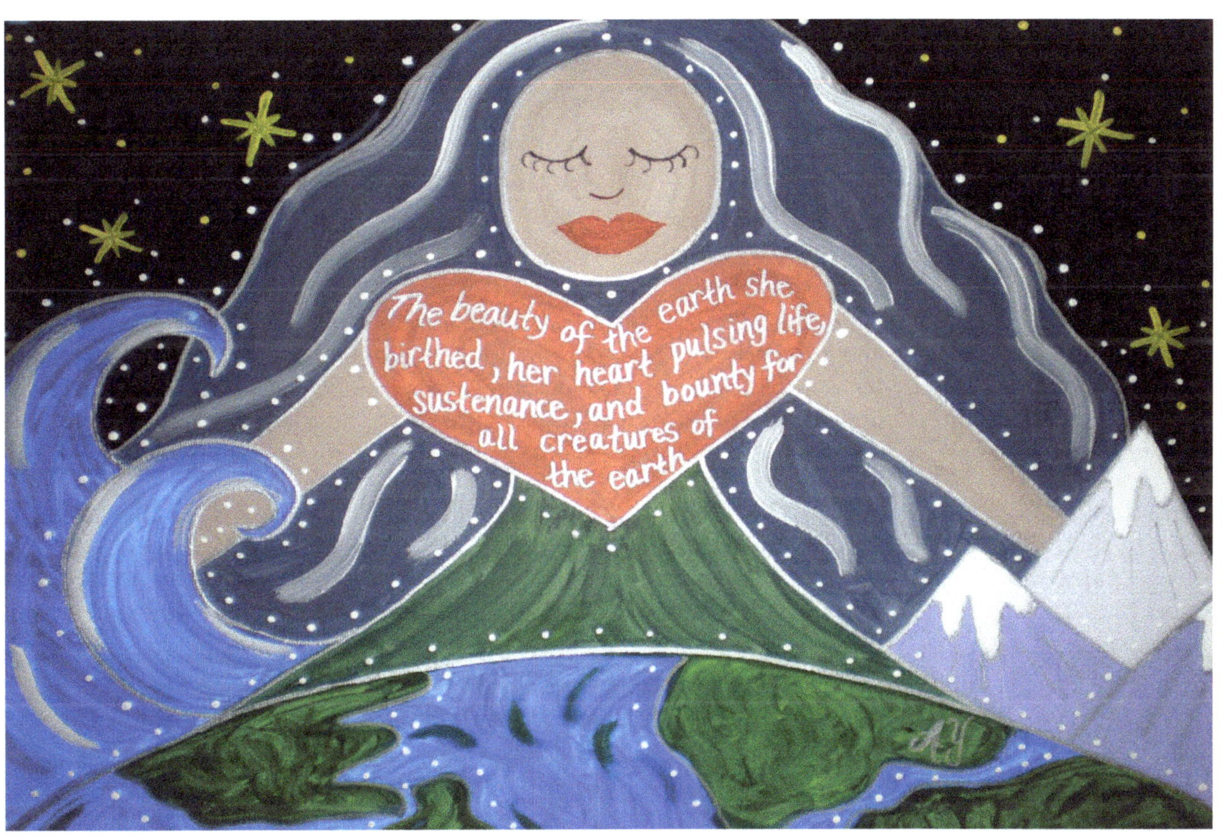

Gaia
Acrylic on Canvas, 16x20

Gaia

Similar to Pachamama is the myth of Gaia. Gaia is the goddess or personification of Earth in Greek mythology. She reigns as mother of all, responsible for the bounty of the earth. So, as I painted Gaia's icon I knew she must rise up from the earth, and since she gave birth to the skies, seas, and mountains, she is also surrounded by the skies, with the waters to her right and the mountains to her left. Many also claim that the mountains are emblematic of Gaia's breasts. But I also knew that, like Pachamama, her heart must be brightest of all. As she reigns over nature, her heart beckons us to wonder:

The beauty of the earth
She birthed,
Her heart pulsing life, sustenance, and bounty for
All creatures of the earth…

Gaia comes from the Greek for "earth" and she considered the most ancient Greek goddess. The daughter of Chaos, mother of the sky (Uranus), the sea (Pontus), the mountains, and several monstrous creatures, Gaia is a rare goddess that births the world into being without the help of a male consort. She has prophetic powers often recounted by the Oracles of Delphi and Olympia. In fact, the Oracle at Delphi—whose very name means "womb of the earth"—is dedicated to Gaia's honor. In classical Greek mythology, she is often portrayed with a cornucopia, which signifies the earth's bounty and fecundity.

Many claim that prepatriarchal societies worshiped Gaia by having deep reverence for the earth, honoring the environment more than later, male-dominated societies. Indeed, elements of ecofeminism and ecotheology implicitly honor this Mother Earth, Gaia.

The next time you enjoy a sunset, splash in the oceans or rivers, or climb through the mountains, remember the beauty of the earth. Let the power of Gaia embolden us to treat this planet with kindness and respect. Let us gaze in wonder at the majesty, greatness, and awe of both the grandeur and intricacy of the natural world. And let us raise our glasses in honor of these women who bore our world, who bear us, and whose stories make us stronger still.

Questions for Contemplation:
Turning Inward:
What part of the natural world most inspires you?
Turning Outward:
What can you do to ensure that more women can be inspired by the beauty of the earth?

Miriam

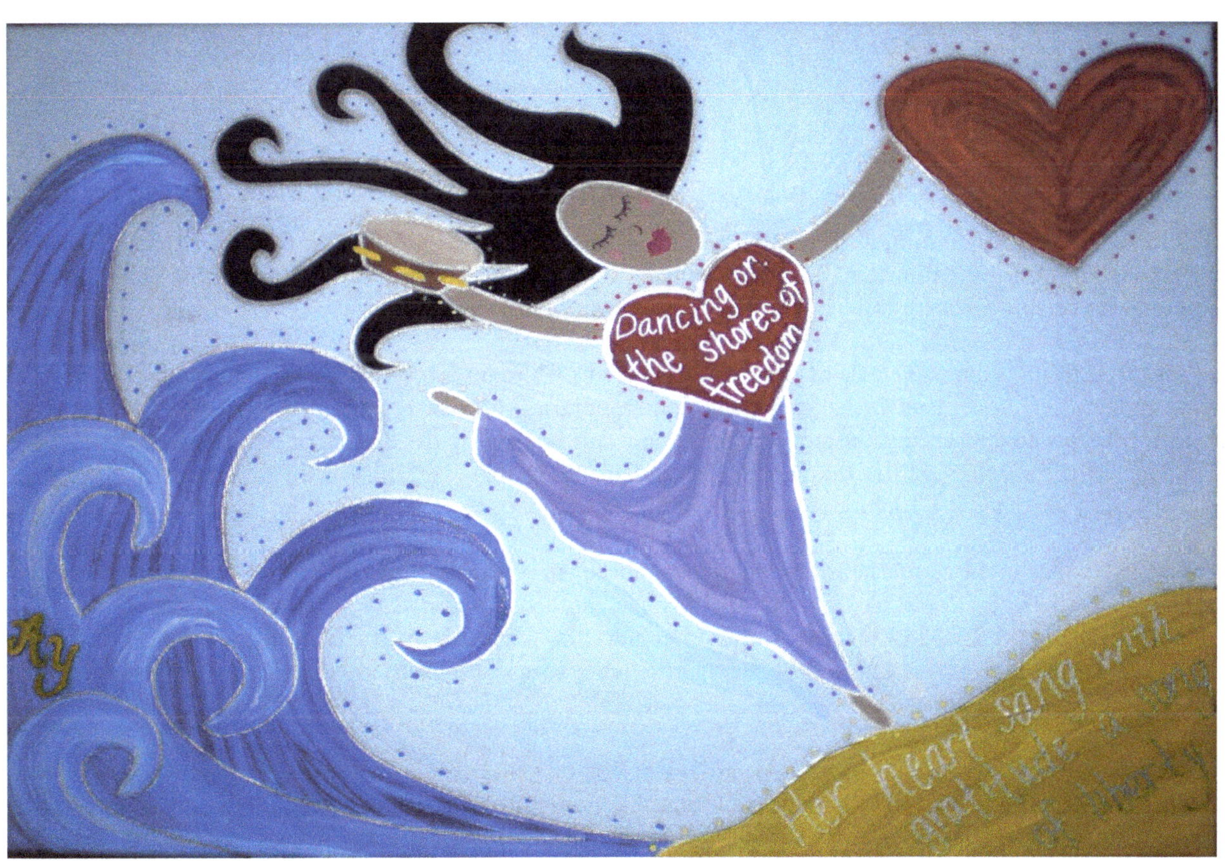

Miriam
Acrylic on Canvas, 16x20, Walker Private Collection

Miriam

We are your subtlest instruments:
no music branches to your breast
that does not sound in us,
no music dies away from you,
that in us lives not,
and even in your absence
your cadence journeys…

Allen Mandelbaum, *Chelmaxioms*

The path to freedom is often muddy. Water sloshes through your sandals and the soles of your shoes stick, clinging to the past, weighing down the future. No one said dancing in wet sand was easy. But it is very holy. Just ask the brave prophetess who celebrated liberation by dancing on the shores of a reedy sea.

Often relegated to the submissive role of sister, the character of Miriam is typically overshadowed by the triumphs of her younger brother. Like many of her canonical contemporaries, Miriam receives little attention in scripture. Her name is only mentioned twice and the story of her song is left unsung by the writers of Exodus. Yet she is there, her song hidden in the crevices of the canon, her dance demanding that we notice the ritual event of liberation, her courageous voice prophesying, leaving a legacy for all the dancing women who will follow in her intrepid food steps.

The story of Exodus involves the Israelites living in bondage, slaves to the Egyptians. We often remember Moses as the prophet who sets his people free. Scrambling through the desert with weary eyes set on freedom, his staff parts the sea of reeds and the Israelites make it to the other side (the tragic fate of the Egyptians chasing said Israelites is another topic for another time). The waters part. Those who were once slaves are now free. Moses for the win! But what of Miriam?

It's interesting to note that before Moses—or any male, for that matter—is dubbed a "prophet," Miriam bears the title. "Prophetess." The first in all of scripture. During the moment of liberation, Miriam is the one who receives this honor, not Moses. The fact that this detail went unnoticed by patriarchal writers and redactors tells me that Miriam's role in the Exodus event is probably much bigger than we originally imagined.

And it's also worth noting that, at the moment of liberation, when the captors are hot on their heels, Miriam chooses to pause and lead the Israelites in a ritual. She sings and dances, her hand-drum the opening drumbeat in a march toward freedom. She inaugurates a liturgical event, her body and voice proclaiming liberatory praise. And all the Israelites follow her example. Can you picture it? Feet still muddy. Sweat dripping from their brows. Water lapping behind them. In that moment of liberation, Miriam chooses to dance. She chooses to sing. She chooses to stop and mark this event as something holy, something set apart, something special.

For years to come, women will follow in her dancing footsteps. In fact, it became an Israelite custom for women to exit the doors of their homes with songs and dances after war. We, too, follow in her dancing footsteps. In those moments of liberation, Miriam reminds us to pause and ritually mark our new-found freedoms. When we find ourselves on the shores of freedom, Miriam reminds us to lift a song of praise and a dance of gratitude.

As she leaps from the waters of bondage onto the shores of liberation, her heart and her hand-drum accompany her as she cries out to us:

Dancing on the shores of freedom
Her heart sang
With gratitude
A song of liberty.

We remember you, Miriam, when our muddy feet dance toward liberation. We remember you when our once-silenced voices sing the songs of freedom. Even in your absence, your cadence journeys.

Questions for Contemplation:
Turning Inward:
In what ways are you in need of liberation?
Turning Outward:
What can you do to help liberate women who are still oppressed, enslaved, and marginalized today?

Saraswati

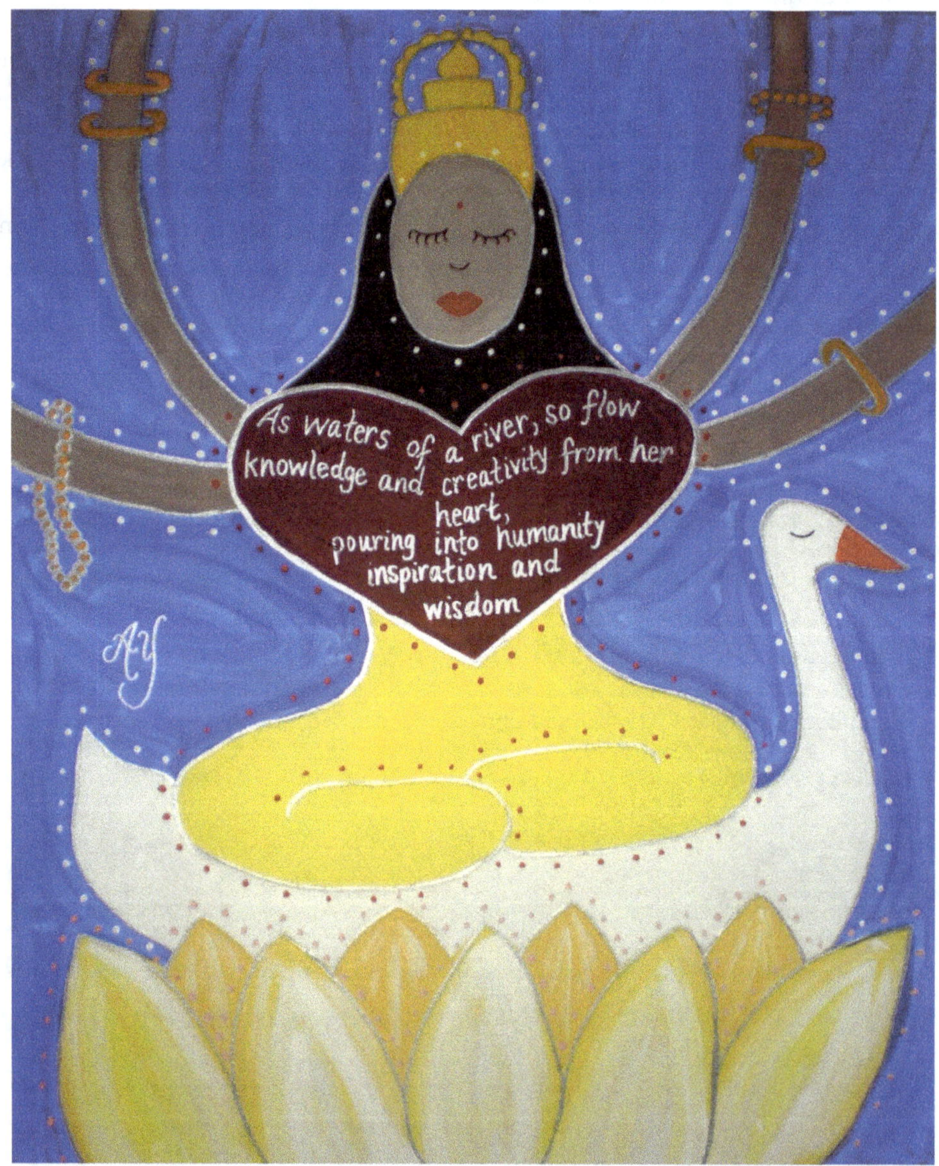

Acrylic on Canvas, 16x20

Saraswati

I was precariously perched atop a file cabinet tacking a giant cloth to the wall when another staff member entered my office. "What's that?" she asked, puzzled, and pointing to the massive cloth now covering my wall. "Saraswati," I responded, hopping off the file cabinet, "the Hindu goddess of arts, creativity, and learning." She raised her eyebrows. "Our previous Baptist preacher didn't have any Hindu goddesses hanging on the wall," she said with a wry smile. "I guess I'm not your average Baptist preacher," I chuckled.

For years I have been searching for Saraswati, claiming her as my patron saint, the one who guides my path as I navigate three seemingly disparate callings: artist, scholar, and preacher. In Saraswati, these three callings merge. Naturally, I hang a giant image of her on my office wall and wear a pendant bearing her likeness around my neck. She reminds me that the divisions between fields are our construction; that academics can be creative, art can be holy, and preaching can engage the mind. These three seemingly disparate callings do not have to be mutually exclusive. Saraswati certainly wouldn't see them this way.

Saraswati (Sarasvatī) is the Hindu goddess of knowledge, music, arts, and science. Along with Lakschmi and Parvati, she is part of the trinity of consorts with Brahma, Vishnu, and Shiva. Often depicted on a river or body of water, her name literally means "she who has flow." Hindus pray to Saraswati for creative inspiration and academic knowledge, but most importantly for divine knowledge essential for reaching *moksha*, or liberation. Her iconography is riddled with symbolic meaning. Iconographically, her four arms represent the four aspects of human personality: learning, mind, intellect, and alertness. Her white pearls represent the power of meditation and spirituality; her pot of water represents the creative mind and powers of purification; her *veena/vina* (type of guitar) represents the perfection of all arts; and her book is the sacred *Vedas*.

Because her iconography is well-established, years passed before I decided to paint my own icon depicting her image. While she embodies so many aspects of life that are vitally important to my calling, I felt as though it wouldn't be right for me to paint her in my own style. The list of my Holy Woman Icons grew as more and more women that I admire filled empty canvases with color, beating hearts, and inspiration. I continued to feel as though someone was missing: Saraswati. As I prepared for a solo art show at a gallery "by women and for women," I knew that Saraswati needed to join my other Holy Women.

Seated on both the swan and lotus that often accompany her, and surrounded by the deep blues of flowing water, Saraswati spread her four arms wide, embracing all. Her heart cries out to us:

As waters of a river,
So flow knowledge and creativity
From her heart,
Pouring into humanity
Inspiration and wisdom…

The ways in which Saraswati embodies the arts, knowledge, and spirituality in her unified and flowing being continues to inspire and challenge me to live fully into these seemingly disparate elements of my own life and calling. Because, once upon a time, before academics created fields and relegated certain questions as only answerable by particular experts, and before we divided science from religion and lost our innate sense of wonder, and before creativity and the arts were dubbed "soft" and "un-academic," Saraswati reminded us that the arts, knowledge, and religion are inextricably linked.

So, this goddess, who hangs on the office wall of a Baptist preacher, reminds all of us to make connections otherwise unseen. Her creative heart inspires us to search for and create beauty. Her wisdom emboldens us to ask difficult questions that may not have easy answers. And the ways in which this goddess connects knowledge and the arts with religion is very holy indeed. May we do likewise.

Questions for Contemplation:
Turning Inward:
How are the arts, knowledge, and spirituality connected in your own life?
Turning Outward:
What can you do to help others make these vital connections?

Salome

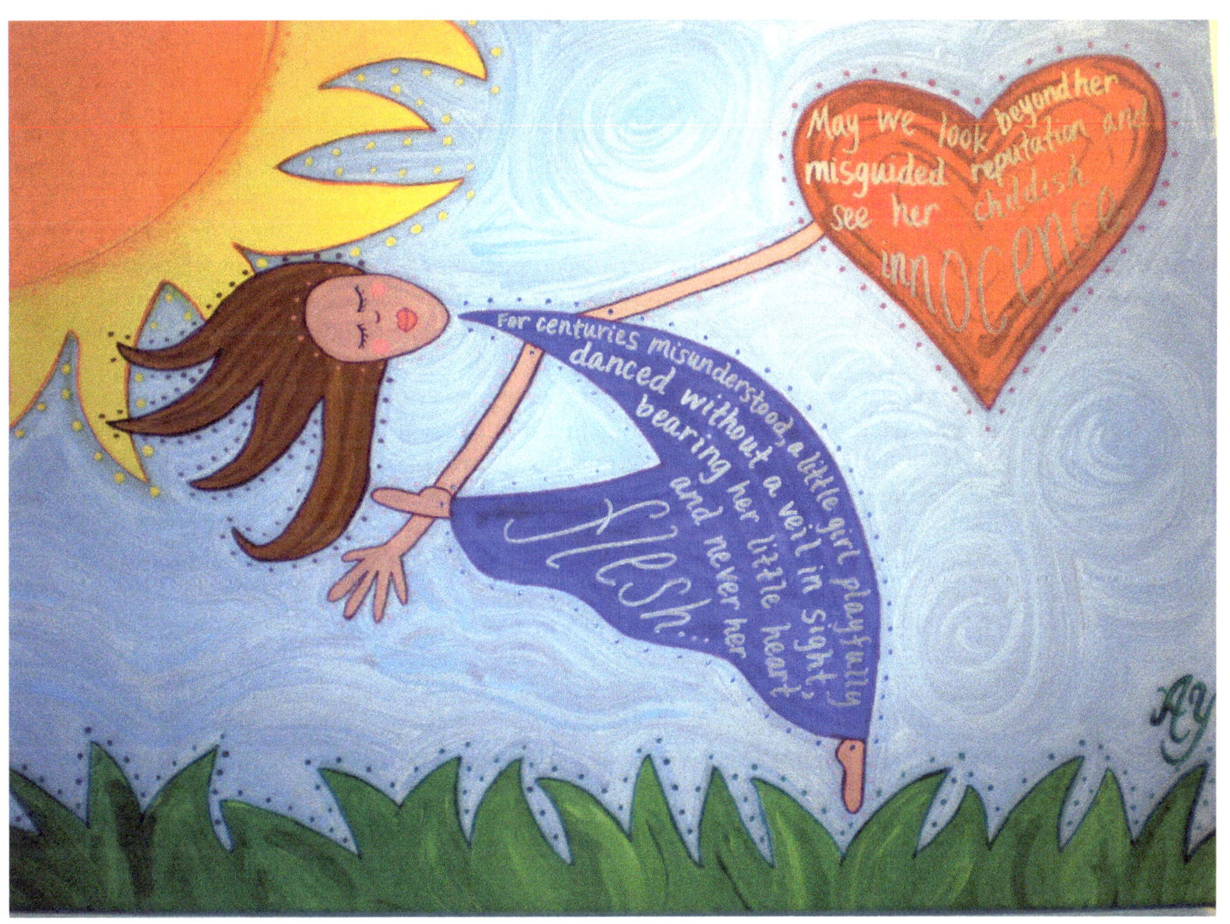

Salome
Acrylic on Canvas, 16x20, Carter Private Collection

Salome

If you carefully read Mark 6:17-29 or Matthew 14:3-11, you're probably wondering why this icon features someone named Salome. There was no mention of anyone named Salome in the text. Rather, in the Markan text both the dancing daughter and her mother are named Herodias. In Matthew's text, the daughter is nameless. It wasn't until later when Josephus, a Jewish historian, named her Salome and stated that she was responsible for the beheading of the John the Baptist.

Since Josephus made up her name, interpreters have gone crazy with blame, ruining the poor little girl's reputation. The more prominent John became in history, the more infamous Salome became. This is reflected in art, as well. In 1462 we have Gozzoli's rendering of Salome, which shows the dance of an innocent child doing gymnastics and twirling the way many little children do when given the spotlight. Perhaps Gozzoli translated Greek in addition to producing famous paintings, because it's clear that the word used to described "Salome" is *thugater*, which means "little daughter." Based solely on what the text says, and even these early artistic renderings, it's obvious that this scripture is about a little girl dancing for play and fun and then being taken advantage of by a conniving mother and uncle.

We wonder, then, why Salome gets such a bad rap. I've heard many avid church goers point to Salome when describing why they don't want dance in worship. Additionally, I recall a male seminarian claiming that Salome might as well have had a pole to swing from because she was so much like a stripper. You see, with the development of the femme fatale in 19th and 20th century art, film, and literature, Salome's story was quickly exaggerated. Gustave Moreau painted over 100 images of Salome in the 1870s, all illustrating a seductive woman in gauzy fabric. Then Oscar Wilde wrote his infamous play, *Salome*, and it is clear that he never bothered to even read the accounts from the Gospels because his play includes an adult Salome flirting with John the Baptist, stripping down to a dance of seven veils, and then kissing the severed head on a bloody platter in 1894. So much for the text describing Salome as a "little daughter."

Then performing artists went wild (pun intended) with the story. Richard Strauss composed an opera, Loie Fuller and Maude Allan choreographed dances that are little more than a strip tease as they embody the "dance of seven veils." Amidst it all, a little girl's reputation is destroyed and dance is demonized as nothing more than an agent of seduction and slander. In these ways, popular culture impacts our understanding of Salome's dance even more than the bible does!

If we chalk the plays, the opera, the paintings, and the choreography up to extreme poetic licensing, then perhaps we can return to the heart of the text. And we'll see the story of a little girl who was asked to dance by a family member at a party. I have many such memories from my own childhood as I cried "Watch me! Watch me!" to parents, aunts, uncles, and grandparents while I leapt and twirled, filled with the child-like innocence that we adults often forget when it comes to worship. I am convinced that Salome's dance was no different.

Salome's dance is most often vilified as a twisted erotic dance of desire. But, as we have seen, this interpretation does not cling to the heart of these scriptures. Rather, our readings of the text have been colored by culture, art, and the bias of patriarchal commentators over the centuries. One can only wonder if the stories would be received differently if the genders were reversed. What if little boy Herod danced before Queen Salome? Would artists, commentators, and culture have interpreted their tale differently?

All of my Holy Women Icons are my way of seeking redemption: for the viewer or for the woman depicted. In the case of Salome, her reputation has been so maligned over the centuries that the little girl's playful dance steps are forgotten. Salome's character must be redeemed. So, I knew that Salome must be depicted as a playful young child in the most innocent of settings. As little girls throughout history have danced for family members and friends, so too does Salome dance, her heart crying out for understanding:

For centuries misunderstood, a little girl playfully danced without a veil in sight,
May we look beyond her misguided reputation and see her childish innocence

So, the next time you see a woman depicted as a dangerous femme fatale, or hear an ill-advised seminarian refer to a child's dance as that of a seductress, I urge you to harken back to the text. Translate it yourself. Redeem history. And listen to the misunderstood stories of dancing girls all over the world.

Questions for Contemplation:
Turning Inward:
In what ways has your reputation been misunderstood or misrepresented?
Turning Outward:
In what ways have you misunderstood or misrepresented others? How can you change this?

Sojourner Truth

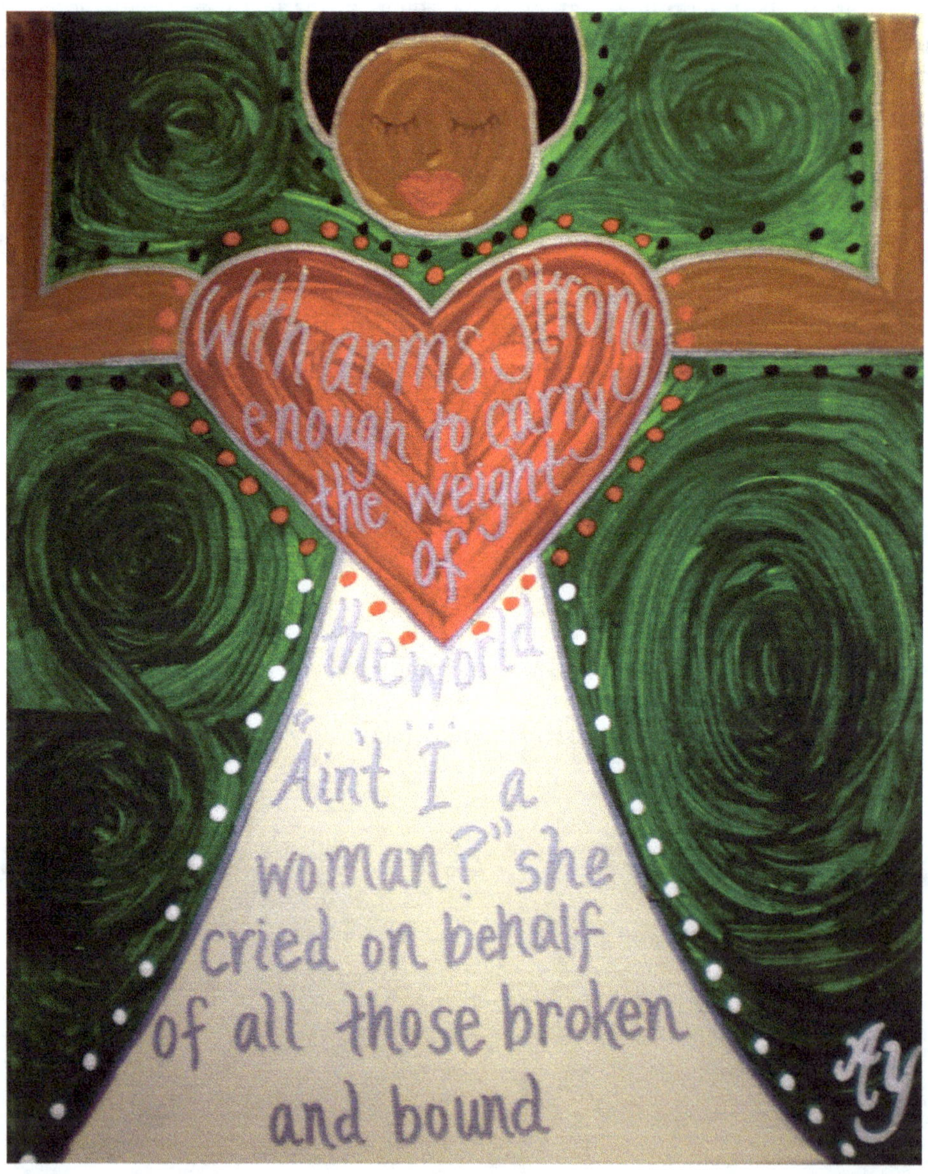

Sojourner Truth
Acrylic on Canvas, 11x14, Carter Private Collection

Sojourner Truth

When studying the story of Sojourner Truth, I am reminded of the importance of Jacquelyn Grant's work on womanist Christology. In *White Women's Christ and Black Women's Jesus*, Grant overviews the contribution of white feminists to the so-called problem of Jesus' maleness, while beginning to construct a womanist response to this incarnational conundrum. She states, "It is my claim that there is a direct relationship between our perception of Jesus and our perception of ourselves (Jacquelyn Grant, *White Women's Christ and Black Women's Jesus,* 63)."

Beginning with Mary Daly, feminists have responded to Jesus' maleness in a variety of ways. Daly argues that because the person of Jesus is male, the male is recognized and celebrated as the superior being. In these ways, the maleness of Jesus is something to be rejected or exorcised because Jesus' understood gender identity contributes to patriarchy and does not hold salvific power for women. Rather than rejecting Jesus altogether, Rosemary Radford Ruether asks the foundational question, "Can a male Jesus save woman?"

Jesus' gendered identity is an issue of incarnational theology because, according to the Christian tradition, God had to become human. So, God became flesh, just like you and me. But God did so in the person of Jesus, a male who appeared to fall into one side of the constructed gender binary, the side that has power and privilege. So, Ruether's question begs us to consider how one whose gendered body is afforded power and privilege can relate to those without power and privilege. Grant notes that for white feminists, "the doctrine of Christology, from its initial formulated inception has been problematic for women…the fact that the church teaches that God's incarnation is uniquely represented in the historical male figure Jesus, provided for the predominance of the one-sided Christological interpretation throughout the history of theology (Grant, 83)."

Feminists like Letty Russell respond to Ruether's question through a liberation perspective by highlighting Jesus' universal participation in the new humanity. The maleness of Jesus is known as the "scandal of particularity" because his gender was constructed in a particular way. Russell notes that Jesus had to have been a man simply because of the patriarchal context in which he was born; his message would have been lost if Jesus was born into the body of someone gendered female. So, Russell challenges women to disconnect Christ's work from his maleness. Jesus' gender, according this perspective, is not as important as his message of liberation and salvation. Therefore, the maleness of Jesus is merely incidental. The humanity of Jesus, however, is salvific.

In contrast, Rita Nakashima Brock does *not* think that a male Jesus can redeem woman, saying:

> If Christology is to be reclaimed in feminist visions, the image of an exclusive divine presence in a 'perfect' man called Jesus who came to be called the Christ is disallowed. The doctrine that only a perfect male form can incarnate God fully and be salvific makes our individual lives in female bodies a prison against God and denies our actual, sensual, changing selves as the lover of divine activity (Rita Nakashima Brock, "The Feminist Redemption of Christ," in *Christian Feminism*, ed. Judith Weidman,68.)

Brock proposes that Jesus, and his maleness, be decentralized in the Christian tradition so that the stories and experiences of women can come to the center. Still, Elizabeth Johnson revises traditional Christological understandings of Jesus by deeming him Jesus-Sophia, speaking about how wisdom is made flesh in the person of Jesus. This wisdom-in-flesh liberates what has previously been twisted into justification for patriarchal domination.

Grant critiques these views by highlighting the way many white feminists have presumed a sisterhood of experience based on gendered oppression, while neglecting or ignoring the way women of color have also experienced oppression based on racialized identity. She explains that Jesus is understood in diverse ways in the womanist community, but primary is the notion of Jesus as a co-sufferer. In this way, Jesus understands what it's like to be oppressed and marginalized.

Before Alice Walker ever coined the term "womanism," an abolitionist and women's rights activist who escaped slavery articulated poignantly this Christological debate and the ways white feminists ignored the plight of black women. At the 1851 Ohio Women's Convention, Sojourner Truth raised her voice to proclaim one of the most nuanced and powerful "sermons" about incarnation ever uttered:

> Then that little man in black there, he says women can't have as much rights as men, 'cause Christ wasn't a woman! Where did your Christ come from? Where did your Christ come from? From God and a woman. Man had nothing to do with Him. If the first woman God ever made was strong enough to turn the world upside down all alone, these women together ought to be able to turn it back, and get it right side up again! And now they is asking to do it, the men better let them. (Sojourner Truth, "Ain't I A Woman," in *Feminism*, ed. Schneir, 94.)

Grant nuances this beautiful argument further, noting that today, the Christ who is found in the experiences of black women *is* a black woman. Jesus is incarnate, gendered, and racialized as a black woman (Grant, 220). Or, as many thoughtful theologians have proclaimed, Jesus was a male, yes, but the Christ could be a woman. In this case, Christ is incarnate as a black woman.

Sojourner Truth stands tall, proud, and strong, her heart crying out to us:

With arms strong
Enough to carry
The weight of the world…
"Ain't I a woman"
She cried on behalf
Of all those broken and bound.

The powerful words proclaimed by Sojourner Truth, and highlighted in Grant's book, remind us that many women have important contributions to make to theology, but their voices often go unheard due to the privileges and oppression associated with race, class, gender, sexuality, ethnicity, and ability.

Questions for Contemplation:
Turning Inward:
How does the concept of a male savior impact your own spirituality?
Turning Outward:
In what ways have you ignored the contributions of women who are from oppressed groups because of their race, ethnicity, religion, ability, or sexuality? How can you change this?

The Shulamite

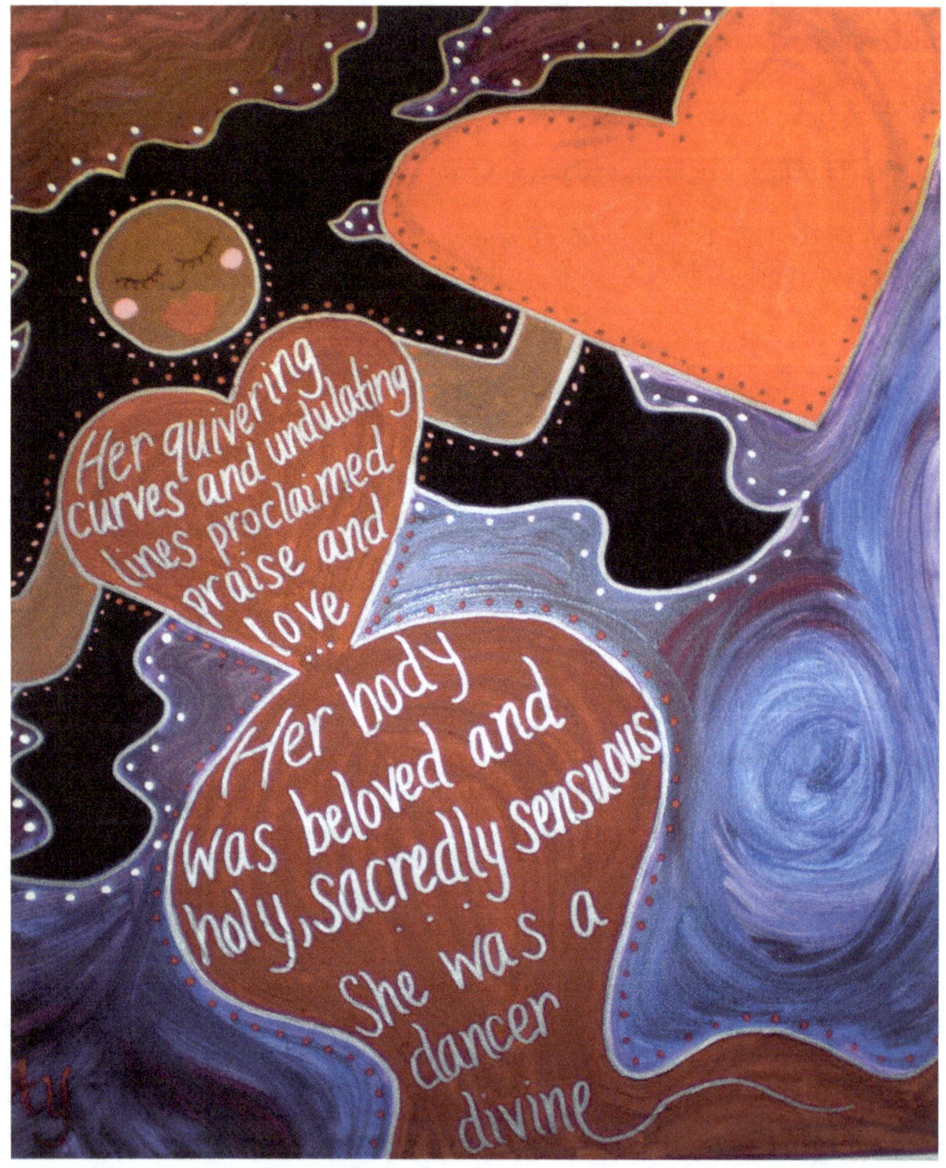

The Shulamite
Acrylic on Canvas, 16x20

The Shulamite

The Shulamite is a dancer made famous by the erotic love poetry dedicated to her sensuous curves in Song of Songs:

Return, return, the Shulamite.
Return, return, and let us gaze on you.
How will you gaze on Shulamite in the dance of the two camps?
How beautiful are your sandaled feet, O prince's daughter.
The curves of your (quivering) thighs like jewels crafted by artist hands.
Your vulva a rounded bowl; may it never lack wine.
Your belly a mound of wheat hedged by lotuses.
Your breasts like two fawns…
(Song of Songs 7:1-4 translation mine)

I first encountered the Shulamite in a passing reference by dance historian Wendy Buonaventura. She listed the Shulamite as an example of a bellydancer in the Hebrew bible. It was only an example, merely an item on a long list of historical references. Nonetheless, this brief mention was enough for me to translate the text, embark on an exegetical adventure, and begin to ask questions about the movement vocabulary embedded in the Hebrew.

The words describing the Shulamite are commonly understood as a traditional Arabic love poem called a *wasf. Wasfs* are intended to describe female beauty and are found in two additional locations in Song of Songs. What is striking about this particular *wasf* is that it describes the Shulamite from toe to head, which is opposite of traditional *wasfs*. Feminist biblical scholar Athalya Brenner proposes that the reason for this descriptive reversal is due to the fact that the lover—whom she assumes is male—is teasing the Shulamite for having a pudgy stomach; therefore, she surmises that it is a parody of a *wasf.* Brenner contends that the male lover is doting upon the Shulamite's beautiful dancing legs (which are also rotund) and then shifting to poke fun of her jiggling belly.

While this is a possibility, I find that other comparable *wasfs* and the role of bellydance offer an alternative interpretation. Within this *wasf* category, there are strikingly similar bodily description poems, such as the tale in *Thousand and One Nights*:

> The…damsel…was the loveliest creature Allah had made in her day, and indeed she outdid in beauty all human beings…her middle was full of folds, a dimpled plain…and her navel an ounce of musk, sweetest of savour could contain. She had thighs great and plump, like marble columns twain or bolsters stuffed with down…and between them a somewhat, as it were a hummock great of span of a hare with ears back lain…and indeed she surpassed…with her beauty and symmetry. (Translation taken from Brenner, *I Am*, 165-6)

In both *wasfs* we read the description of a beautiful woman, a woman with "curved" or "plump" thighs, a rounded "vulva/navel." Her belly is like a "mound of wheat" or "dimpled plain," that is "full of folds." In bellydance quivering bellies, trembling thighs, shaking buttocks, and shuddering breasts are precisely the point. Hip shimmies, rib cage isolations, and abdominal rolls are part and parcel of bellydance's movement vocabulary. The intention of the dance is to make these parts of the body—the stomach, breasts, hips, and butt—tremble, quake, roll, shake, shimmy, bounce, and jiggle. To a dance historian, it is clear that the movement being described in the *wasf* is bellydance.

What is more, the history of bellydance provides a fascinating lens for deciphering the gender of the Shulamite's lover. Historically, bellydance was performed by and for women only; men were not permitted. It was either a dance form celebrated in all-female groups in homes or within the confines of all-female harems. In such harems, women were "set apart" from men and lived, learned, and loved within the harem. Women often learned to read, write, play musical instruments, and dance in these harems. Bellydance often provided women with an opportunity to explore their sexuality, staging imitations of the sex-act or engaging in same-sex love. Because of the queer history of bellydance, one cannot help but deduce that the Shulamite's lover may have been another woman, delighting in same-sex love.

This dancing history combined with feminist and queer understandings of the Song of Songs in a way that enlightened my approach to painting the Shulamite as a Holy Woman Icon. Calling the Shulamite holy is my way of affirming female sexuality, the beautiful variety of the body's shapes and sizes, and including the LGBTQ community in the canon of saints. Accordingly, the Shulamite's robust curves fill the canvas as we remember her dancing body:

Her quivering curves and undulating lines
proclaimed praise and love…
Her body was beloved and holy,
sacredly sensuous…
She was a dancer divine

So, love your body. Celebrate your flesh. Dance. Like the Shulamite, your body is like a jewel, crafted by artist's hands.

Questions for Contemplation:
Turning Inward:
How might you honor and treat your body as though it is crafted by artist's hands?
Turning Outward:
What can you do to honor and treat others as though their bodies are also crafted by artist's hands?

Virginia Woolf

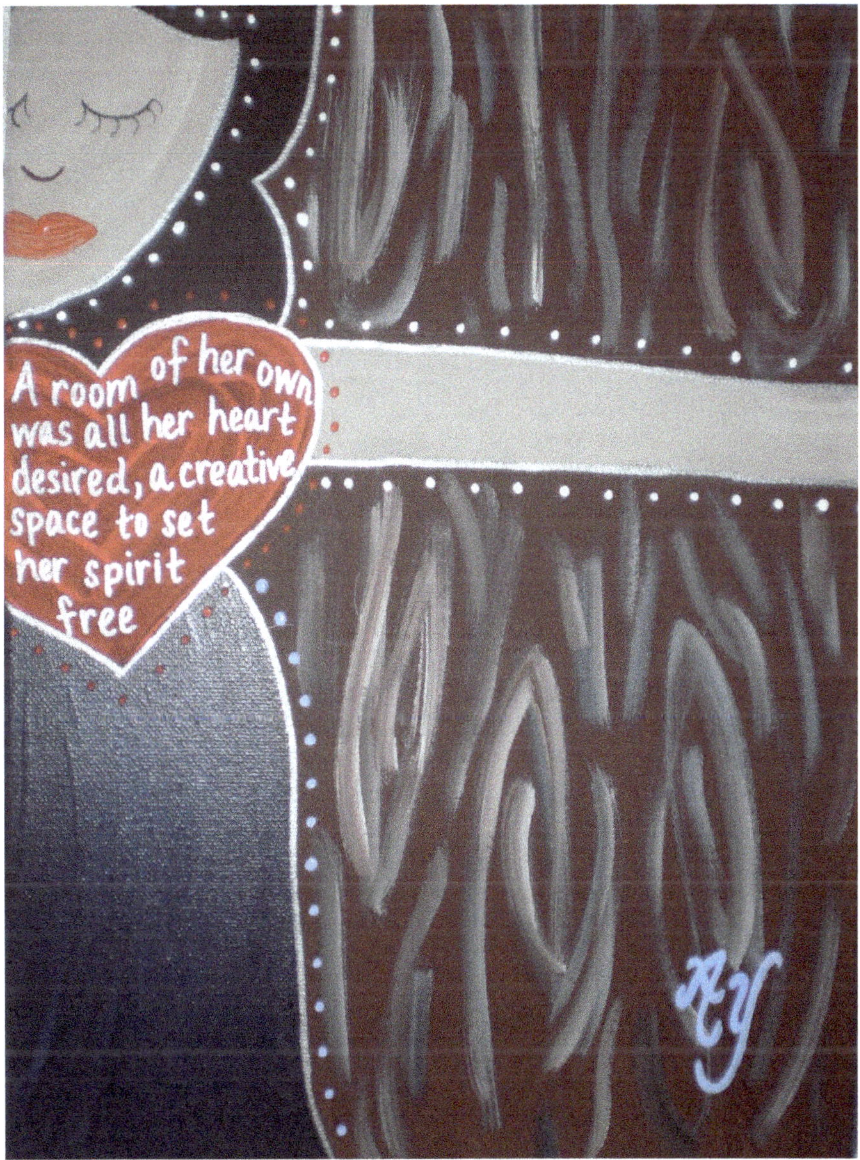

Virginia Woolf
Acrylic on Canvas, 11x14

Virginia Woolf

I first encountered her in the lyrics of a song. The Indigo Girls shaped my adolescence, molding me into a young feminist as I sang in harmony with other teenage girls:

They published your diary
And that's how I got to know you
The key to the room of your own
And a mind without end

And here's a young girl
On a kind of a telephone line through time
And the voice at the other end
Comes like a long lost friend

So I know I'm alright
Life will come and life will go
Still I feel it's alright
'Cause I just got a letter to my soul

Emily Saliers and Amy Ray (the Indigo Girls) were singing about Virginia Woolf, naming the song after her. As I belted out the lyrics with my soon-to-become-feminist friends, I had yet to learn who Virginia Woolf was and how her life and work had shaped my own. All I knew as I harmonized those many years ago was that this woman must be special if the Indigo Girls dedicated a song to her. I felt a longing to know her, to learn more about her, for her to call me on that telephone line through time and tell me I'm alright. Joining the ranks of my other Holy Women Icons, Virginia Woolf is a novelist, one of the greatest writers of the twentieth century.

Virginia Woolf (1882-1941) is most famous for being a respected novelist during a time when women were not welcome in the academy as writers. *Mrs. Dalloway*, *To the Lighthouse*, *Orlando*, and *A Room of One's Own* have no doubt led countless young women to claim their self-worth, spark their creativity, and dare to dream big.

It was her book-length essay, *A Room of One's Own*, which emboldened me to live into my calling. So, I knew that her icon must pay homage to this particular work. "A woman must have money and a room of her own," Virginia Woolf wrote. Certainly such a sentiment is not without flaws. Some have called it classist, highlighting the countless creative, talented, brilliant women around the world who will likely never have access to such a room, yet still manage to produce meaningful poetry and prose. I'd like to hope that, instead of merely referring to a literal room, Woolf may have also believed that every woman deserves to have an emotional, mental, and spiritual space that is safe, empowering, and free. I cannot help but think of the many times I penned my own writings, not in a beautiful studio with a view, but on public transportation, on the back of a napkin, or with my laptop precariously balanced on my lap in a crowded space.

As I painted her icon, I knew that "the room of one's own" must engulf more space on the canvas than she did, her heart beating in the room and outside of it, and her arms outstretched as though she is inviting other women into the room. So, she stands on the edge where she belongs, her heart telling us:

A room of her own
Was all her heart desired,
A creative space
To set her spirit free

As I painted, of course, I listened to the Indigo Girls. Together we sang, "If you need to know that you weathered the storm of cruel mortality, a hundred years later I'm sittin' here living proof." As feminist writers, painters, singers, artists, activists, and scholars unite in spaces of freedom—rooms of our own—we are living proof that what Virginia Woolf did mattered. In these ways, she gave us all a space to call our own.

Questions for Contemplation:
Turning Inward:
How can you create a "room" of your own, a space to practice creativity, affirmation, and spirituality?
Turning Outward:
What can you do to create "rooms" for women without access to the privileges and luxuries you have so that they may also have safe spaces to practice creativity, affirmation, and spirituality?

La Negrita / Virgen de los Angeles

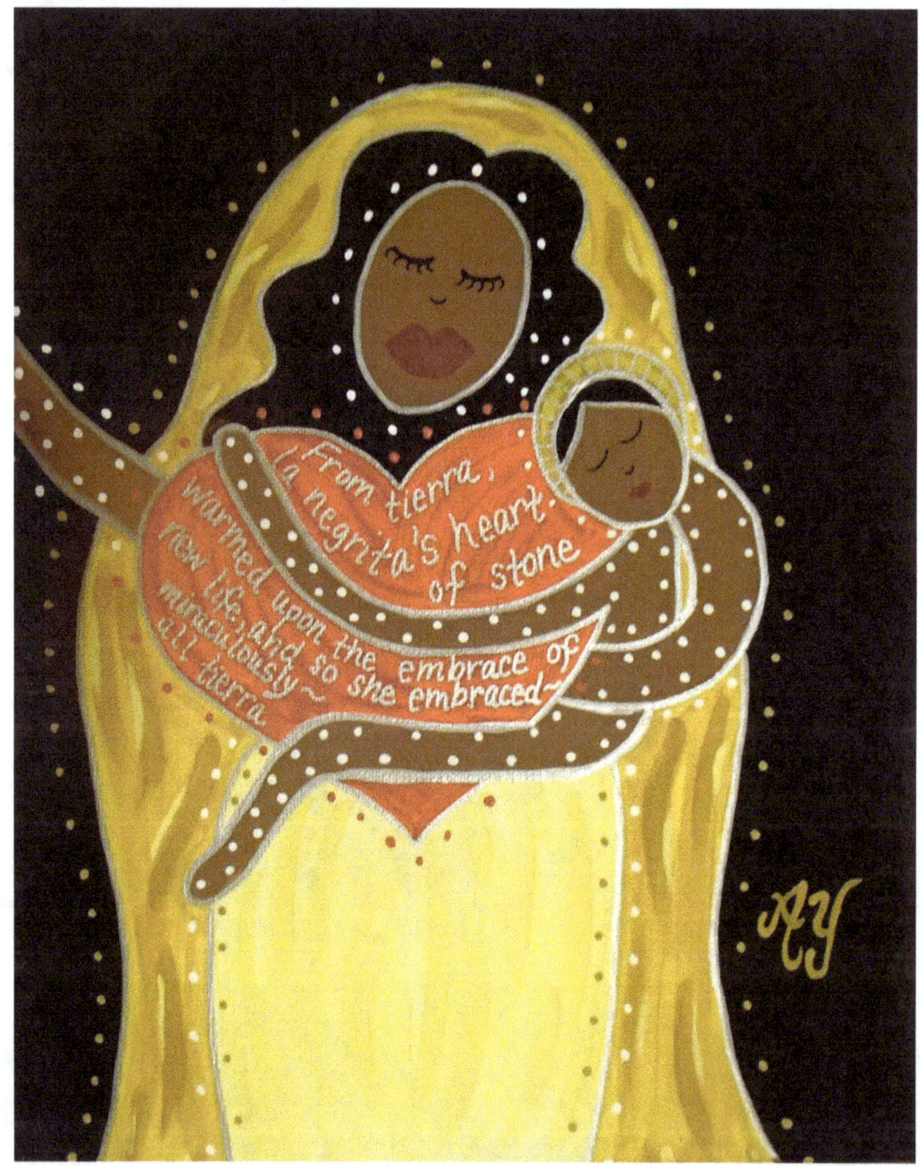

La Negrita
Acrylic on Canvas, 11x14, Arce Private Collection

La Negrita / Virgen de los Angeles

Every year thousands of Costa Ricans make a pilgrimage to visit their patron saint on August 2. Some penitents walk the 22 kilometers on their knees from the capital of San José to the Nuestra Señora de los Angeles Basilica in Cartago where the small statue of La Negrita is now on display.

Also known as La Virgen de los Angeles, the Black Virgin is a very small representation of the Virgin Mary. She was originally discovered by an indigenous woman on August 2, 1635. When the poor indigenous woman tried to take the stone statuette, it miraculously reappeared. The people responded by building a shrine around her.

One may wonder where La Negrita came from and why this wondering woman tried to keep her. Legend has it that she came from stone, dark earth, *tierra.* Like the indigenous woman who discovered her, she represented the people of her homeland, indigenous Costa Ricans whose voices were often unheard. Like the anonymous indigenous woman who discovered her, she took up little space in the world, for she was only a tiny black stone less than a meter tall. As the Black Virgin is small in stature, the woman who first bore witness to her was small in society, relatively powerless, her body and being viewed as less-than. In these ways, La Negrita's small and earth-bound stature evokes the people she represents.

What is more, though La Negrita may be small in stature, she works big and powerful miracles, often for the poor and marginalized. This is why so many Costa Ricans pilgrimage to her to request miracles and healing. It may also be why she is now dressed in an extravagant gold dress and standing upon a jeweled pedestal in the basilica. While some feel that such extravagance detracts from her humility, others claim that by elevating La Negrita's dress and stature, all indigenous women are elevated, redeemed, and made a bit more holy and worthy.

I knew little of La Negrita when I was first commissioned to paint her. I knew she was part of the wider spirituality of La Morenita—the little dark one, the syncretized, often dark-skinned Mary—similar to Our Lady of Guadalupe and in stark contrast to elements of colonized Marian spirituality. Since I had the tremendous privilege of being commissioned to paint La Negrita by a brilliant scholar who resides in the borderlands as a half Costa Rican and half Salvadoran feminist, I was fortunate to learn, not only about La Negrita's story, but of my dear friend and colleague's story. Amidst our conversation and my research, I reread much of Gloria Anzaldúa's work, contemplating mestiza consciousness, borderlands, and mujerista theology.

Like Anzaldúa and the colleague who commissioned this icon, I wanted to blend Spanish and English, acknowledging the constant flux of borders and cultures embodied in La Negrita's being. I thought of Anzaldua's *Una lucha de frronteras*/A Struggle of Borders:

Because I, a *mestiza,*
continually walk out of one culture
and into another,

because I am in all cultures at the same time,
alma entre dos mundos, tres, cuatro,
me zumba la cabeza con lo contradictorio.
estoy norteada por todas las voces que me hablan
simultáneamente.

"I am all the voices that speak to me simultaneously." I thought of Anzaldúa and I thought of *tierra. Tierra* is a Spanish word with multiple connotations, ranging from homeland, native land, earth, or even dirt/soil/earth. In these ways, *tierra* is like an intentional pun that has multiple meanings that aren't easily translated into English. I thought about how La Negrita comes from *tierra*—a small black stone that's part of the earth. She embraces all *tierra*—working miracles for all people from across the land. And Costa Ricans travel across *tierra*—their native land—to reach her.

And I thought of my brilliant friend and colleague. In many ways she is a lot like La Negrita: small in stature, living at the borderlands, traveling across *tierra* between Costa Rica and the United States, yet she does big, miraculous, and wonderful things. As I stretched my canvas to paint La Negrita, I thought of these things. I knew I wanted to portray her in elements of her original form, particularly with a toddler Jesus wrapping her tiny body. Engulfed in black earth, yet shimmering bright, her heart is largest of all and it cries out to us:

From tierra, La Negrita's
Heart of stone warmed
Upon the embrace of new life,
And so she embraced—miraculously—
All tierra

La Negrita's powerful presence reminds us that no matter how small, how forgotten, how minimized our presence on this dark brown earth may be, we have the capacity to do miraculous things, good things, compassionate things. Like La Negrita, may we embrace all, warming hearts of stone into hearts that beat with love for all the earth, for all *tierra.*

Questions for Contemplation:
Turning Inward:
Has there been a time when you felt too small or powerless? What empowered you?
Turning Outward:
How can you better acknowledge those who are treated as small and powerless in our society? How can you better honor their place on the earth?

Mother Teresa

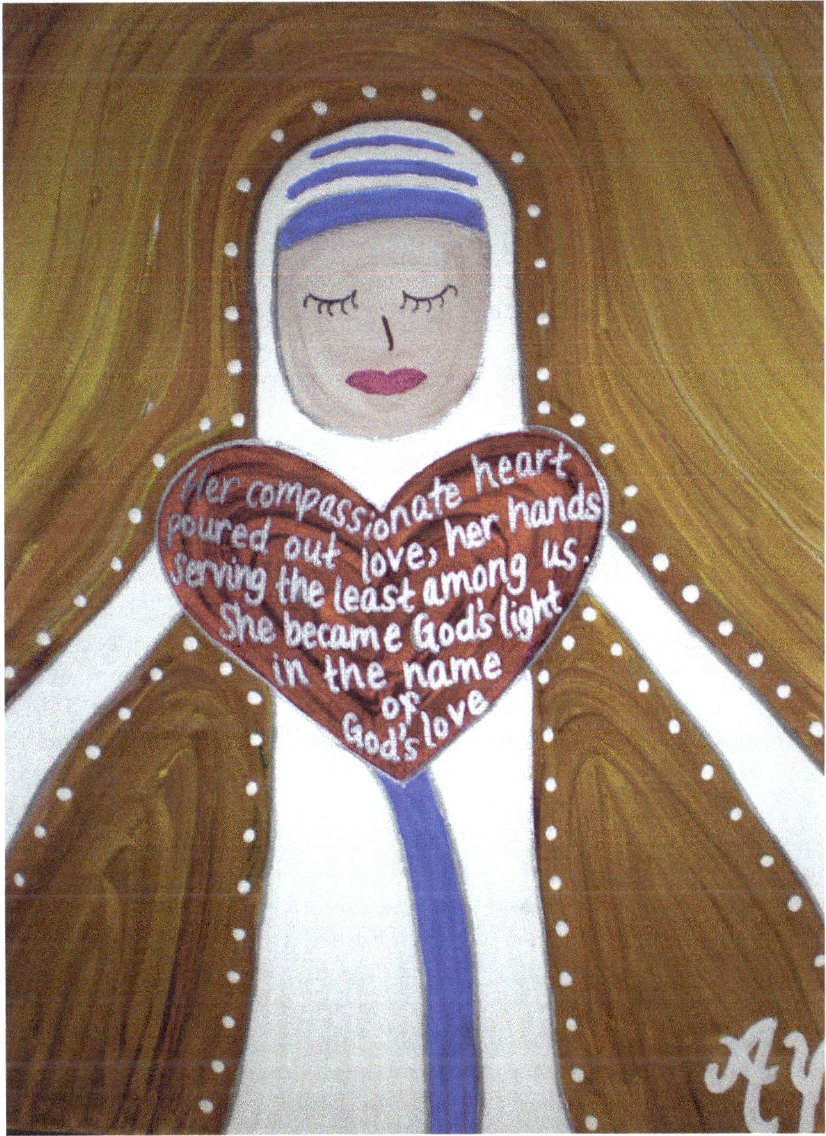

Mother Teresa
Acrylic on Canvas, 11x14, Donze Private Collection

Mother Teresa

Of all my Holy Women Icons, Mother Teresa joins Mary in being one of the most familiar, and often the one least cited for the cause of feminism. When I first began the Holy Women Icons project, she was an obvious woman who came to mind, but I resisted painting her for several years. Perhaps it's because her story is so familiar. Maybe it's because this pillar of humility and service embodies so many virtues that have been used to oppress women for centuries. I cannot quite articulate my resistance, but it was real.

So, when I was commissioned to make this holy woman an icon, I knew that it was incumbent upon me to remember Mother Teresa's story. Born in August of 1910 as Anjezë Gonxhe Bojaxhiu to Albanian parents, the soon-to-be-sister would become the most prominent woman Catholic in the world, embodying the virtues of humility, servitude, and compassion. Upon taking her religious vows to become a nun, she chose to be named after Thérèse de Lisieux, the patron saint of missionaries. Her service was to the poor and marginalized in India, her heart so devoted to Indians that she became a citizen in 1948.

Around the time Sister Teresa became Mother Teresa, she received permission from the Vatican to start the diocesan congregation that would later become the Missionaries of Charity, her order. The year was 1950 and she wanted an order, a congregation whose mission was to care for "the hungry, the naked, the homeless, the crippled, the blind, the lepers, all those people who feel unwanted, unloved, uncared for throughout society, people that have become a burden to the society and are shunned by everyone." Taking very seriously Jesus' admonition to "care for the least among us," the Missionaries of Charity began as a small order with only thirteen members in Calcutta. By the time she died in 1997, the order had grown to more than four thousand sisters serving in orphanages, AIDS hospices, and refugee centers that care for the blind, aged, disabled, poor, homeless, victims of natural disasters and famines, and individuals struggling with substance abuse. When Mother Teresa spoke of creating an order whose mission was to care for all those people who feel unwanted, she meant it. It was not only her prayer. It was her actions, her livelihood, her vocation, her calling.

Today the Missionaries of Charity has over 4,500 sisters and is present in over 100 countries. Members of the order must take vows of poverty, obedience, chastity, and "wholehearted free service to the poorest of the poor." Because of these selflessly admirable works, Mother Teresa was awarded the Nobel Peace Prize in 1979. The awards committee stated that she was worthy of the prize "for work undertaken in the struggle to overcome poverty and distress, which also constitutes a threat to peace." Never one for ostentation or glamour, she accepted the award, but only without the ceremonial banquet; she also asked that the nearly $200,000 prize be given to the poor in India. It is no surprise, then, that she has not only been canonized by my brushstrokes and dubbed a Holy Woman Icon, but she is also on her way to sainthood within the Catholic Church. In 2003 she was beatified "Blessed Teresa of Calcutta," which is the third step toward becoming a saint.

While Mother Teresa is certainly respected for her charitable work and compassionate heart by a vast array of people from myriad traditions, her life is not without controversy. Many feminists have widely criticized her for her public campaigns against contraception, which coincides with Catholic social teaching. Others have claimed that the conditions in her hospices are not up to current standards. Though I do not agree with her stance on issues of contraception and sexuality, I cannot help but respect, admire, and honor the tremendously gracious, kind, and compassionate life she lived. Like many of my other Holy Women Icons, one does not have to affirm every element of a woman's life to recognize her holiness.

Mother Teresa's commitment to the least among us reminds us of the vital importance of intersectionality. Transnational feminists in particular claim that the fight for equality and liberation for women intersects with the fight for equality and liberation for persons of color, the poor, and other disenfranchised groups. In these ways, addressing and overturning sexism is just as important as addressing and overturning racism, classism, heterosexism, ageism, ableism, and all the other "isms" that oppress and marginalize. So, while her public stance against contraception may conflict with the overall cause of feminism, her laudatory work to help all humanity thrive certainly makes her an icon of compassionate kindness for all women.

It is remembered that Mother Teresa once said, "By blood, I am Albanian. By citizenship, an Indian. By faith, I am a Catholic nun. As to my calling, I belong to the world. As to my heart, I belong entirely to the Heart of Jesus ("Mother Teresa of Calcutta," *Vatican News Services*)." And it is to her heart that I turned when painting her.

Because her white sari with blue stripes is how we identify her, I wanted her to be dressed in this traditional garb. Like all nuns, the intention is for her heart and actions to shine more than her clothing. She stands small, but centered on the canvas, her arms outstretched, reaching down to the lowest in an embrace as her heart cries out to us:

Her compassionate heart
Poured out love, her hands
Serving the least among us.
She became God's light
In the name of God's love.

No matter how one feels about the Catholic Church or her views on contraception, your heart cannot help but expand when imagining the life Mother Teresa lived. It was a life dedicated to feeding those who are hungry, welcoming those who are excluded, holding those who have never been held, and providing love and care for those who have been rejected and excluded. If this is not the aim of feminism, I'm no longer interested in being a feminist. She was a holy woman, indeed.

Questions for Contemplation:
Turning Inward:
How can you better follow your own calling to share love and compassion with others?
Turning Outward:
What material possessions prevent you from living simply? Might you give some of these possessions away to the poor?

Lottie Moon

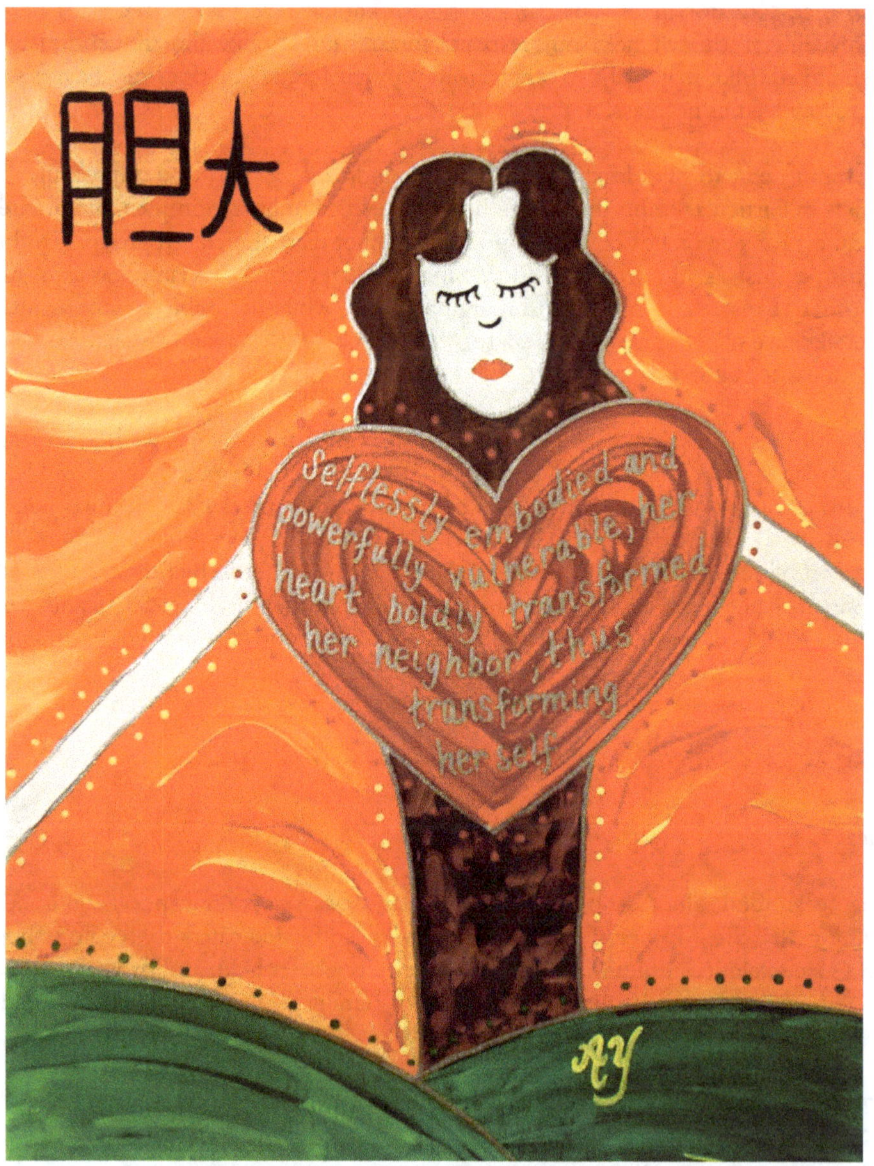

Lottie Moon
Acrylic on Canvas, 11x14, Hasty Private Collection

Lottie Moon

I never imagined I'd paint her. Though I was not raised in church, I have vivid memories of worshiping in Southern Baptist Churches, churches where women's voices were not permitted behind the pulpit, churches where women could never dream of ordination, churches that damned LGBTQ folks to hell with a pound of a fiery fist on a well-worn bible perched atop an angry pulpit. Canonize a Southern Baptist woman into the sainthood of Holy Women Icons? No, thank you.

Though I am an ordained Baptist minister myself, it's important to remember that there is a vast spectrum of belief and practice when it comes to the Baptist church. Because our polity is non-hierarchical and we are anti-creedal, one cannot easily say, "All Baptists believe ______ or all Baptists practice _______." Whether you are as conservative as the Southern Baptist Convention or as liberal as the Association of Welcoming and Affirming Baptists, we all share some core Baptist distinctives: the separation of church and state, believer's baptism, the autonomy of the local church, freedom of conscience, and the priesthood of all believers. Learning of these distinctives as a young feminist searching for a faith to call my own, I was immediately drawn to the core Baptist tradition. They reject hierarchy. All are supposed to be equal. It is up to the individual conscience to determine what one believes. And it is up to the individual church to determine how that particular community of faith will practice those beliefs. It is feminist to its core. Southern Baptists feel otherwise, which is why they refrain for ordaining women and claim that they should be submissive to their husbands.

So, when a friend and colleague who attended seminary with me wanted to commission an icon to inspire her daughter, Lottie Moon's namesake, I was skeptical to say the least. Much like with Mother Teresa, I was concerned that canonizing this seemingly holy woman would elevate attributes that have been used to oppress and marginalize women for centuries. Because I trust this friend and colleague, I decided to set my preconceived notions aside and listen. I listened to why this feminist mother thoughtfully and intentionally chose to name her first child, her beloved daughter, after Lottie Moon.

Like me, this new mother has a love/hate relationship with the Southern Baptist Church. She loves elements of her childhood and family that were nurtured there, but she rages against the way the SBC treats women today. But she's always loved Lottie Moon's story. Born in December of 1840, Charlotte Digges Moon, "Lottie," said and did things unheard of for women of her era. At a meager four feet and three inches tall, she followed a call from God to go to China as a missionary, an occupation rarely afforded women in the Baptist faith—or any faith—during this time. She began her mission in China with appalling views of the Chinese people, but over time she allowed herself to be transformed by her neighbors, eventually embodying Chinese culture and identifying herself with her neighbors. She came to believe this so fully that she shared her salary, her food, her whole self with her Chinese neighbors until there was nearly nothing left of her. She died weighing only fifty pounds after giving away all her food to those who were hungry.

This feminist mother is typically quite leery of advocating total self-emptying, but she stated that "Lottie did not seem to do it out of some perverse understanding of holiness. She did it out of intense compassion for her new brothers and sisters. She had become one with them. Their plight was hers. Her resources were theirs." She was a bold and opinionated woman who changed the face of missions and the way women were treated in ministry. Lottie's namesake's mother claims, "I think of her as having the intensity of fire all the way to her bones."

As I listened to my friend, this new mother who named her daughter "Lottie," I thought of a woman who has been misunderstood. Only instead of society and the church being the ones who misunderstood her, lumping her life and story into the category of "other," it was I who had misunderstood. I lumped this brave woman—this bold spitfire who sailed into the unknown to teach and feed and empower other women—into the category of "Southern Baptist" and relegated her to a person unworthy of feminist exploration.

I may not agree with everything about Lottie Moon, I may balk at the notion of trying to "Christianize" a "heathen" people, and I do reject the way Southern Baptists treat women, but there are elements of this tiny woman's life worthy of canonization. Like Mother Teresa, her actions stemmed from a deep sense of compassion for the least among us. She was bold, courageous, fiery, and did more in the world than anyone would have dreamed given her gender, her faith tradition, and her small stature.

As I painted her into sainthood, I knew that I wanted to pay homage to her much loved and respected China. In the upper left corner I painted the character "Dan Da," which is Mandarin for "bold." For years, Lottie Moon studied to learn Mandarin, and this character also has the implications of being a hero or leader that shifts the status quo. Emblazoning the sky around her tiny body are shades of fire—reds, oranges, yellow, and pink—to capture the idea of Lottie being a spitfire. Though I continue to struggle with a self-effacement so deep that one denies one's self even the basic nourishment of food, I made her very thin based on the sacrificial way she gave away her own food to the hungry. Yet, I wanted this little daughter to grow up knowing she could be strong, so Lottie's tiny arms are spread big and wide, as her massive heart cries out to us:

Selflessly embodied
And powerfully vulnerable,
Her heart boldly transformed her neighbor,
Thus transforming herself.

I am still surprised to find Lottie Moon amidst this great cloud of holy women witnesses that surround me. But I am grateful that there is a little girl growing up gazing at Lottie's big, bold heart, knowing that she has the capacity to do big, bold things that can change the world. And I am grateful that her mother taught me to give this misunderstood woman a second chance. May we all be so bold.

Questions for Contemplation:
Turning Inward:
How have you been transformed by those who are different than you?
Turning Outward:
How have you stereotyped or misunderstood others? How can you change this?

Sophia

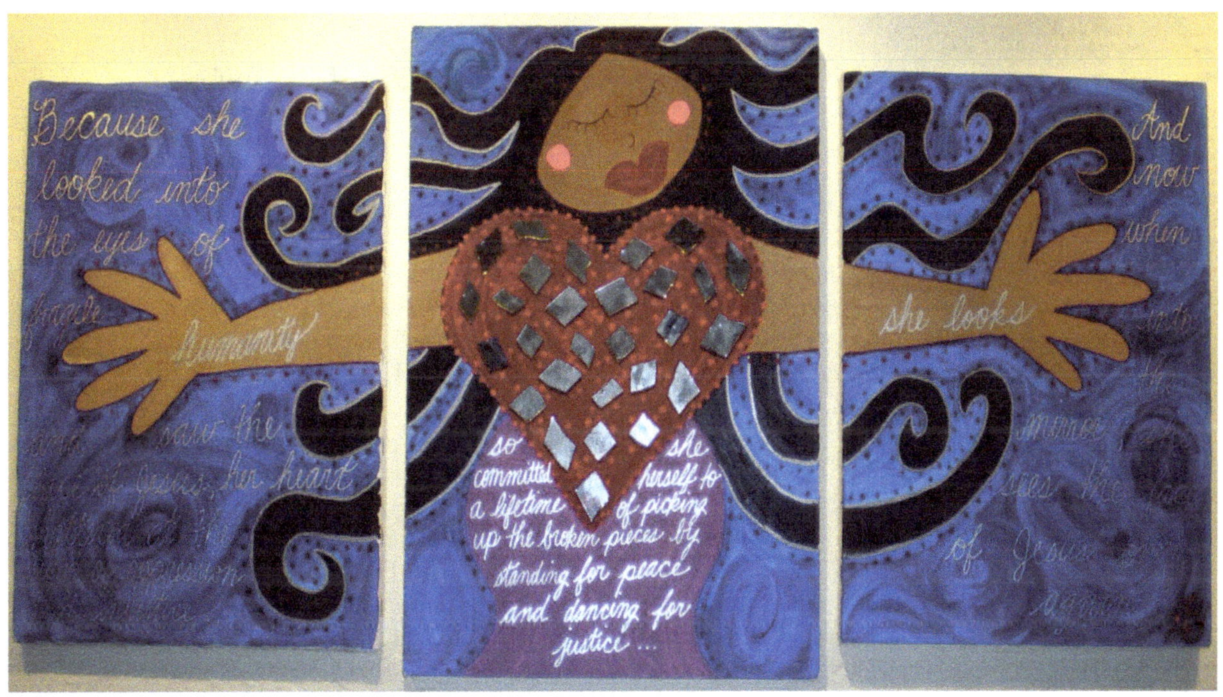

Sophia
Acrylic and Mixed Media on Canvas, Triptych

Sophia

Sophia was the first Holy Woman Icon I ever painted. A church gallery was hosting a Lenten triptych exhibition with the theme of "The Many Faces of Jesus." I knew immediately that the face of Jesus I wanted to portray was Sophia wisdom. *Sophia* is the Greek feminine word for wisdom in the New Testament. Her characteristics are similar to the Hebrew *hokhma*, but expand in early Christian theology as she is understood as a divine attribute, or part of the trinity. In these ways, *sophia* is portrayed as a hypostasis of God's wisdom, or a part of God's substance. Accordingly, early Trinitarian formulas reference God the father, Jesus the son, and Sophia the spirit. A female spirit was undeniably an early part of the trinity.

It is worth noting that such an early understanding of the trinity, and of an unequivocally feminine spirit, was once normative. The Spirit was understood as and spoken of as a "she." April DeConick highlights the difficulty of such an understanding today: "[W]hat must be realized is that Judaism and Christianity are the products of centuries of religious developments. So what might have been considered 'orthodox' at an early time, a few centuries later might be considered 'heretical' because the tradition and practices had drastically changed by then (April DeConick, *Holy Misogyny*, 7)." What was once orthodox—a female *sophia* spirit—has slowly, yet intentionally been overshadowed by patriarchal understandings of the trinity and the spirit.

Feminist theologians, such as Elizabeth Johnson, claim that this Sophia Spirit emboldens the entire trinity—and even all of humanity—to work toward flourishing for all creation. The wisdom of Sophia desires for all people to dwell in places where they can flourish and thrive. Johnson re-imagines the traditional Trinitarian formula of "Father-Son-Spirit" as "She Who Is:" Mother-Sophia, Jesus-Sophia, Spirit-Sophia. This feminine spirit is found in feminist theology and also throughout scripture. The *Gospel of the Hebrews*, for example, records Jesus being taken by the Spirit up to Mount Tabor where Jesus says, "My mother the Holy Spirit took me by one of the hairs on my head and bore me off to the great mountain Tabor." So, the Spirit, *Sophia*, is not simply a feminine Greek word, but Jesus' Heavenly Mother. This early Christian understanding continued in the *Gospel of Phillip*, an early Syriac text. At one point, this early Christian document essentially accuses some early Christians of heresy because they believe that the Spirit is male and that Jesus only has a Heavenly Father when it states, "Some say, 'Mary conceived by the Holy Spirit.' They are wrong. They do not know what they are saying. When did a woman ever become pregnant by a woman?"

And all this was reflected in early church baptismal liturgies, where those being baptized believed that they were entering into the womb of God as they immersed themselves in the baptismal font. In fact, many fonts from the third, fourth, and fifth century are in the shape of a womb. Priests proclaimed prayers, saying, "Blessed are you, Lord God, through whose great and indescribable gift this water has been sanctified by the coming of the Holy Spirit so that it has become the womb of the Spirit that gives birth to the new human out of the old (Sebastian Brock, *The Holy Spirit as Feminine in the Syrian Baptismal Tradition*, 84)."

In fact, the majority of early Christians considered the Holy Spirit to be a feminine attribute of God. Of course Jesus had a heavenly mother and an earthly mother. In fact, Jesus had two moms. What is more, Jesus had two dads. This was normal. Understood. Accepted. Orthodox. For several centuries of Christendom these two moms and two dads comprised the holy family. It wasn't until later when patriarchy crept in ever so smoothly that this orthodoxy became anathema, heresy, wrong.

And now we peel back its sordid history. Scholars translate ancient Syriac and Aramiac texts. Archaeologists uncover baptismal fonts in the shape of wombs. Authors write books that illuminate once-hidden truths. And we see the face of Jesus in the face of Sophia Wisdom. With big, open hands reaching beyond the confines of her canvas and expanding onto either side of the triptych, the wild and flowing hair of Spirit Sophia waves in Dionysian abandon, and we look into her beating heart and see ourselves, our own spirits reflected back at us. And Sophia's heart cries out to us:

Because she looked into the eyes of fragile humanity and saw the face of Jesus,
her heart shattered at the sight of oppression and injustice...
so she committed herself to a lifetime of picking up the broken pieces
by standing for peace and dancing for justice...
and now when she looks into the mirror,
she sees the face of Jesus once again...

Questions for Contemplation:
Turning Inward:
What helps you to best flourish and thrive?
Turning Outward:
How can you help others to flourish and thrive?

Deborah

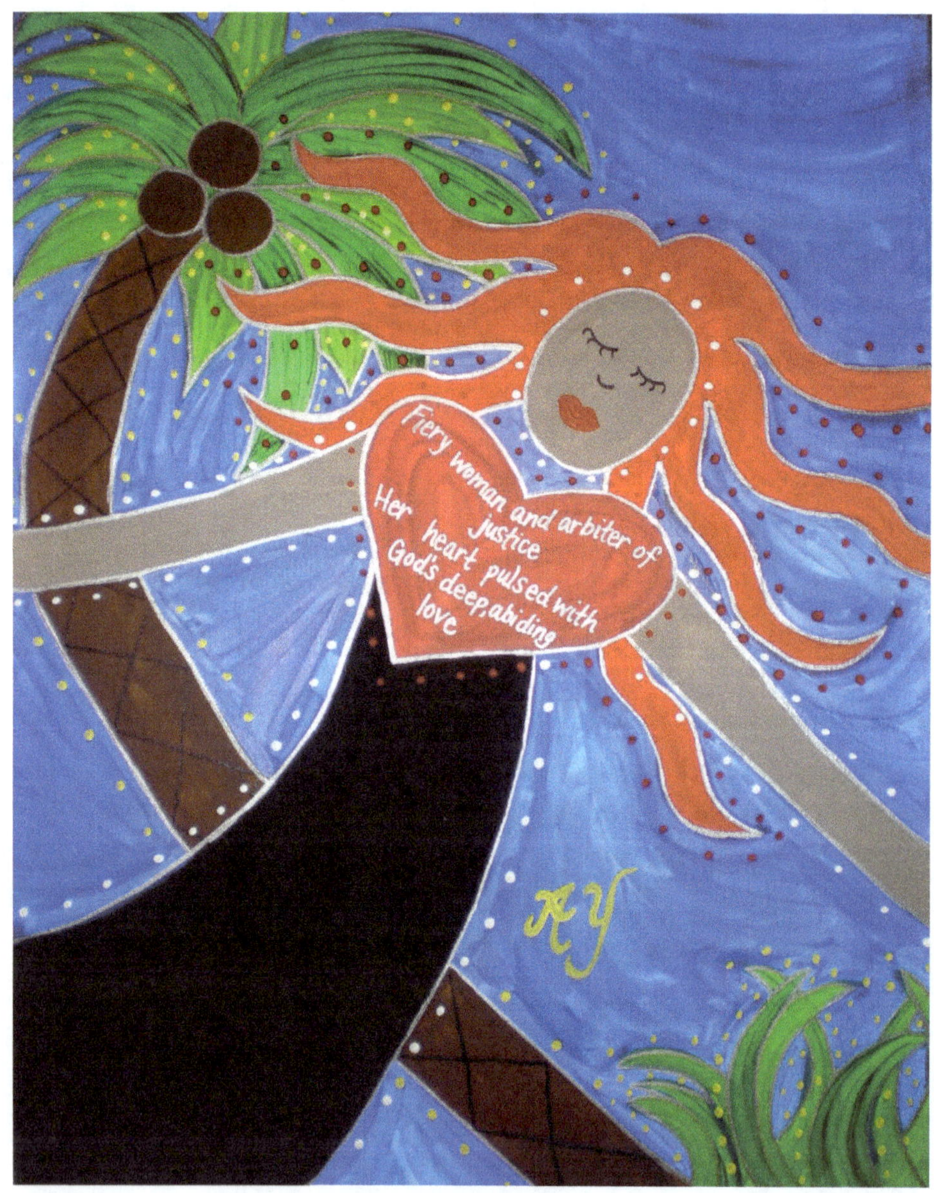

Deborah
Acrylic on Canvas, 16x20, Lynn Private Collection

Deborah

Deborah is one of the few women in scripture depicted as a strong leader who does not need the help of a man. The start to Deborah's story appears bland, a mere introduction to a narrative that will later become juicy, surprising, and even a bit gory. Judges chapter four merely introduces us to a woman named Deborah, a judge over Israel. Judges is a book that records a time when Israel was without a king, so judges had to arbitrate justice, command, lead, and settle disputes. The book of Judges involves a constant downward spiral in which the people of Israel experience God's grace; they forget God and do evil; they get into trouble and cry out for help; a judge arrives to help; the people get better; the judge dies and the people repeat the cycle.

When Deborah appears on the scene, the people have gotten themselves into trouble. We, as readers, know that because she is a judge, she will deliver them. But it's easy to pass over Deborah's uniqueness in reading her seemingly boring introduction. As in most texts, when we take time, we realize there is much more than meets the eye.

The text tells us, "Deborah, a female prophetess, a fiery woman was judging Israel." These facts alone are enough to shock the patriarchal senses of an otherwise oppressive and misogynistic culture. So, we know that the bible was written during a time when women didn't have many rights, and it was edited and canonized in a time when women didn't have many rights. Amidst that patriarchal time of living, writing, editing, and later canonizing, this fiery prophetess and judge survived. That alone is enough give us pause.

But there's more. Most often, the text is translated as "Deborah, wife of Lapidoth, a prophetess, was judging Israel." Because women in scripture are most often named in relation to a man—
wife, mother, daughter—translators assume that Lapidoth is the name of Deborah's husband, even though his name has appeared nowhere else in scripture. Women rarely stand on their own in the bible. Not surprisingly, the word for woman and the word for wife are identical in Hebrew, one in the same. But *eshet lappidot* can also be translated as "fiery woman," "woman of fire," "spirited woman," "woman like a torch." Not merely a wife, Deborah may have been a bit feisty, fiery. Or some scholars contend that this fire-and-torch-like woman may have had red hair. Either way, she stands autonomous as a prophetess and a judge. All her other judging counterparts have been and will continue to be men. Deborah serves as the lone woman who arbitrates justice. According to Susan Ackerman, her titles as judge and prophetess "indicate her role as someone who serves as an intermediary between the human world and the divine (Susan Ackerman, *Warrior, Dancer, Seductress, Queen*, 29)."

Dwelling under a palm tree between Ramah and Bethel, this fiery woman stood for justice, leading her people in a manner unheard of for women. The Song of Deborah in chapter five recounts the ways in which she led the Israelites in battle and is likely the earliest written example of Hebrew poetry. It is the only example that describes a woman as a warrior. Warrior. Singer. Leader. Judge. Prophetess. Fiery woman, indeed. Deborah defied the Israelite paradigm of gender-appropriate behavior by stepping into the traditionally male sphere of leadership. Her gifts of leadership could not be bound by antiquated understandings of women's roles. Her gifts for prophecy could not be bound by oppressive understandings of what it is that women can say and do. Deborah was a judge with unique gifts that were bigger than the opposition that would otherwise hold her captive. Deborah shared her gifts in a way that was uniquely subversive, far from traditional, and of more value than we have the ability to comprehend.

So, it is no wonder that this fiery woman joins my Holy Women Icons. With flaming red hair flowing wildly, befitting of a feisty and fiery woman, she sways underneath an arching palm tree, the bright blue sky big and bold enough for all women who dare to dream as big as this fearless prophetess. With arms reaching out, providing justice for all, her heart cries out to us:

Fiery woman
And arbiter of justice
Her heart pulsed with
God's deep, abiding love

Deborah made the world a better place and I'm convinced that we'd all be better off with some more fiery women in our midst. Spirit, or fire, or whatever you have to offer, be fearless. Be fiery. Be bold.

Questions for Contemplation:
Turning Inward:
What sparks the fire within your heart?
Turning Outward:
How can you be more bold, fiery, and courageous so that others may experience more justice?

Martha Graham

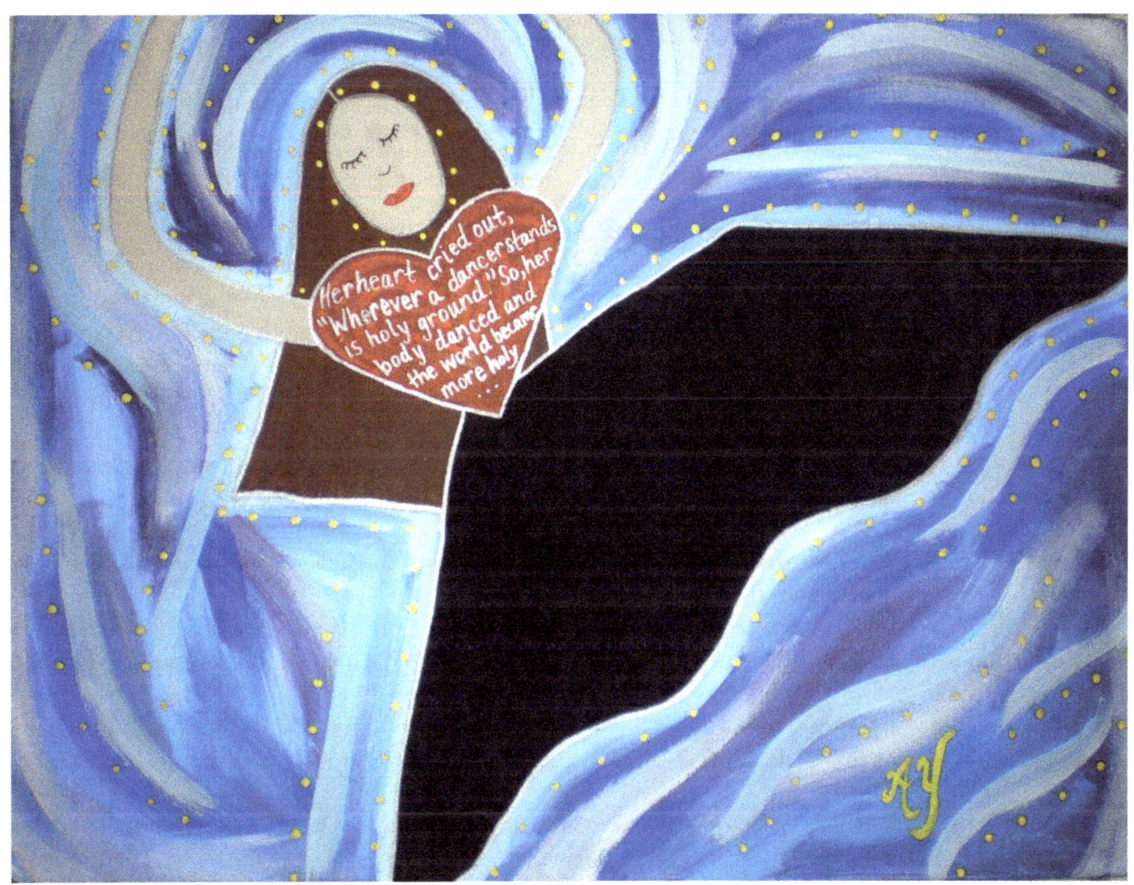

Martha Graham
Acrylic on Canvas, 18x24

Martha Graham

Martha Graham's contribution to the world of dance cannot be overestimated. She is regaled as the Picasso of the dance world, revolutionizing it by introducing an entirely new quality of movement known as modern dance. Not only did Graham revolutionize the dance world, like Isadora Duncan before her, she also made great contributions to feminist spirituality. One of her most famous statements may well have been "wherever a dancer stands is holy ground." Like most dancers who are so in tune with their bodies, Graham new the holiness therein, the ways in which the body can express the ineffable in ways that words alone simply cannot. "The body never lies," she famously reminds us.

Born in May 1894 to a strict Presbyterian family, her first experience of dance was in her family's church. As a 2 year-old child, Graham stepped into the aisle separating the otherwise very still pews of her Presbyterian church and began to dance. It was likely the playful and innocent dance of a child, lacking any inkling of scandal, technique, or even relation to the scripture or overall spirit of worship. Yet it was immediately condemned. Graham was shamed, disciplined, and forbidden to dance in such a place again. Reflecting on her experience from childhood, she remembers: "I was born in Pittsburgh of Scotch-Irish parentage. My people were strict religionists who felt that dancing was sin. They frowned on all worldly pleasures, but were particularly horrified at my showing an early tendency toward an art that seemed grossly sensuous to them. My upbringing led me to fear it myself. But, California swung me the direction of paganism."

When her family relocated to California, Graham's dance training began in earnest. She studied at the newly created Denishawn School of Dancing under the leadership of Ruth St. Denis and Ted Shawn. Their influence would continue throughout her life. Also vitally important to Graham's artistic and spiritual development was Jungian psychology, the writings of Nietzsche, dances and rituals from a variety of Native American traditions, and the mythic work of Joseph Campbell. A voracious reader, Graham claimed that she would be just fine deserted on an island alone as long as she had a dictionary and the bible; she also read virtually everything Joseph Campbell, Jung, or Nietzsche ever wrote, asserting that all of this philosophical and spiritual work were essential to her choreography and artistry.

In fact, she created more than 200 choreographic works with themes of goddess figures, saints, angels, and the Madonna. *Acrobats of God, Adorations, Diversion of Angels, Eyes of the Goddess, Judith, Lucifer, Out of This World, The Plain of Prayer, Primitive Mysteries, Madonna, Seraphic Dialogue, Triumph of St. Joan, Visionary Recital,* and *Herodiade* are just some of the myriad examples of her choreography that feature the sacred, many of which also highlight strong female characters or the feminine divine. *Primitive Mysteries* may be one of her most famous choreographic works. Not only did it feature her newfound technique of curves and angles and simplicity, but it was danced by a group of women, illustrating that women could command an audience's attention without male partners. In her autobiography, *Blood Memory*, Graham reflects on *Primitive Mysteries* and *Heretic,* saying, "I felt at the time that I was a heretic. I was outside the realm of women. I did not dance the way that people danced…In many ways I showed onstage what most people came to the theatre to avoid."

In these ways, dance scholar, Janet Roseman notes that most dance critics have failed to realize that Graham was a foundational spiritual thinker, in addition to being a brilliant dancer and choreographer. About Graham, St. Denise, and Duncan, Roseman asserts, "The fact that all three women created their own schools of training, successfully performed around the world, and ran their own businesses tells us much about their perseverance in a man's domain (Janet Roseman, *Dance Was Her Religion*, xix)." Not only was Graham's work renowned in dance and business, but she entered into the ultimate of men's domains, the church:

> I danced at St. Mark's in the Bowery, a wonderful old church in the East Village set up in the form of an old meeting house. I was in front of the altar rail they had then. I wore a blue dress and I hovered over the crib, which represented the crib of the baby Jesus. The Bishop turned to one of his associates and said, "What is she doing?" And he slowly took off all of his insignia, one by one, the collar, the ring, and so on. All this I could see very clearly as I began my dance. Not exactly a strong confidence builder; it just got me mad. After he watched me dance for a while he put them back on. His disapproval of dance seemed to have ended. He realized I was not going to create a scandal; it was safe to return to being the Bishop. I was all right, I guess. (Graham, *Blood Memory*, 141)

Graham's accolades extend farther than almost any dancer: the U.S. Presidential Medal of Freedom, the artistic emissary for the United States abroad, the first dancer to perform at the White House, Fulbright Fellowships. But I do not iconize her because of her accolades, impressive though they are. I call her a holy woman, canonizing her into folk feminist sainthood, because she honored and the affirmed women's bodies, reminding us all that wherever a dancer stands is holy ground.

Her honored, affirmed, and dancing body encompasses the entire canvas, the classic lines of her modern technique evident in her right leg lifted mid developé, as her heart cries out to us:

Her heart cried out,
"Wherever a dancer stands is holy ground."
So, her body danced
And the world became more holy…

In her 97th year, Graham passed way. When she died she was at work on an unfinished choreographic piece entitled *Goddess*—fitting for this goddess of the dance. About her dance, artistry, spirituality, and choreography, Graham asserted that "you should be ravished by what you see; it should leave a mark on your life." You have ravished us, indeed. For this, the ground upon which we stand is a bit more holy.

Questions for Contemplation:
Turning Inward:
How does your body make the ground more holy?
Turning Outward:
How can you better honor the bodies of others by acknowledging the holiness of the ground beneath their feet?

Maya Angelou

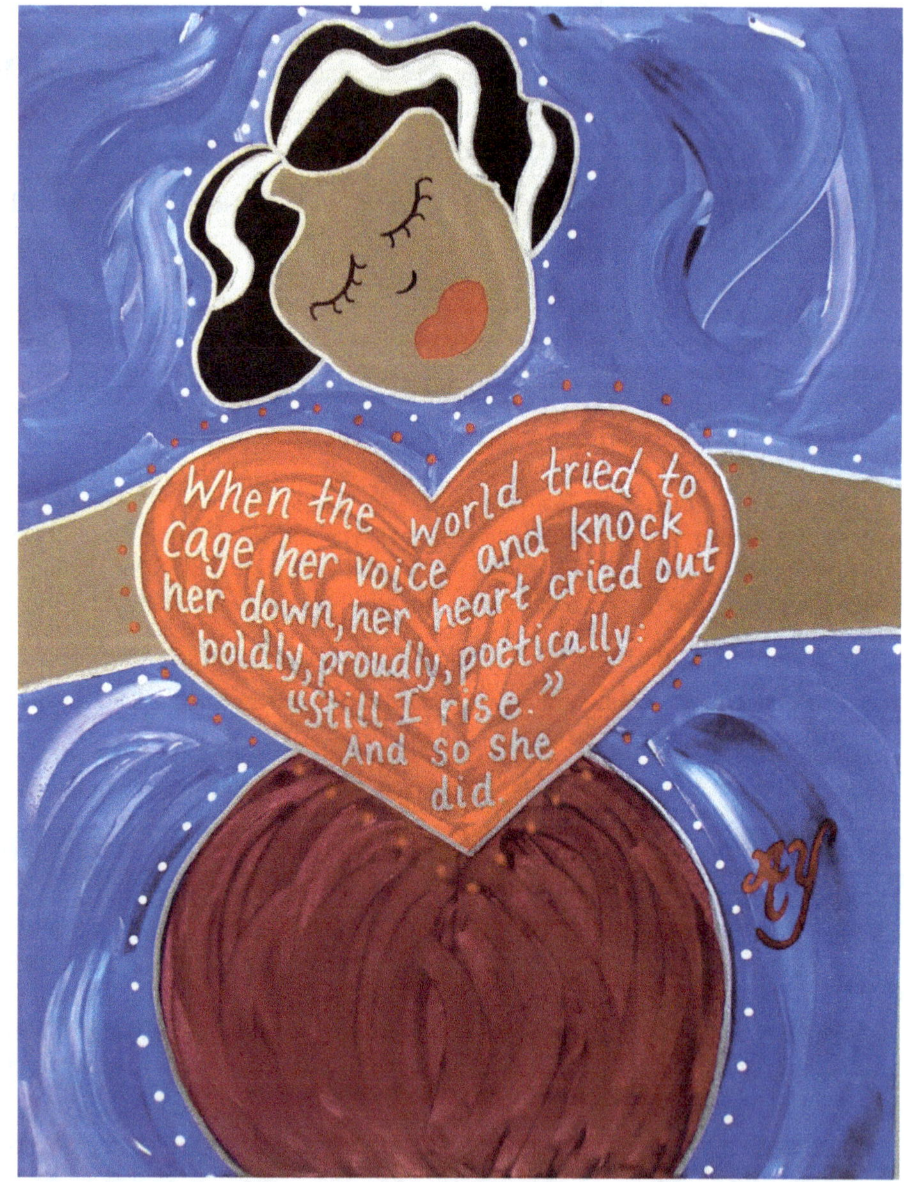

Maya Anglou
Acrylic on Canvas, 11x14

Maya Angelou

Author. Performer. Activist. Poet. Actress. Playwright. There are few others whose accomplishments are as prestigious, prolific, or expansive as Maya Angelou's. I first encountered her work in a ninth grade literature class. The first of her seven autobiographies was our assigned reading. I voraciously consumed every word of *I Know Why the Caged Bird Sings*, my heart filled with grief, my eyes filled with tears, my mind filled with questions. It is no wonder this book is the most acclaimed of all her autobiographies, books of poetry, and essays. As a fourteen year-old my mind was opened to the power of stories, particularly the stories of those vastly different from oneself, and to the oppression black women like Angelou experienced in the United States. As a native white Southerner, *I Know Why the Caged Bird Sings* was my first foray into grappling with the nuances of white privilege.

In college, my creative writing professor packed all ten of the creative writing minors into a van to drive to a neighboring college where Angelou was lecturing. I sat in awe, riveted by every word. And upon the completion of my Ph.D., I moved to Winston-Salem, the place Angelou calls home. I have yet to meet her. If I could, I'd surely hand her the icon I painted in her honor, knowing that my words would fail to express how profound my gratitude is for the work she has done in our world.

This work includes her writing, of course, but also activism alongside both Martin Luther King, Jr. and Malcolm X during the Civil Rights movement, advocacy for women and persons of color, and service as the coordinator for the Southern Christian Leadership Conference. Named Marguerite Johnson on her birth in 1928, Angelou experienced the oppression of being a young black girl in Stamps, Arkansas, and later being sexually abused in St. Louis. She rose up through poverty and prostitution and, in addition to achieving acclaim as a writer, was also an actress, dancer, director, and producer of plays, movies, and television programs.

It is no wonder she has received over thirty honorary doctorates, holds the first lifetime Reynolds Professorship of American Studies at Wake Forest University, was awarded the Presidential Medal of Freedom, and was asked to recite her poem, "On the Pulse of Morning," at the inauguration of President Bill Clinton; she was the first poet to make an inaugural recitation since Robert Frost in 1961. And her writing has arguably expanded the genre of autobiography by focusing on themes of race, family, identity, gender, and travel.

She has taught countless people that all God's children do, indeed, need traveling shoes, that in the face of tremendous injustice, black women still rise, and that beautiful, true, and evocative writing has powerful potential to stir and shake readers. There was no doubt in my mind that Maya Angelou is a holy woman. But it wasn't until I moved to her hometown that I canonized her into sainthood and she officially became a Holy Woman Icon. Standing center and bold, her head gazes slightly down as though she is remembering the powerful story of her life thus far. Her heart is largest of all as it cries out to us:

When the world tried to
Cage her voice and

Knock her down,
Her heart cried out
Boldly, proudly, poetically:
"Still I rise."
And so she did.

The voice and writings of this prophetic poet embolden us all to rise up for justice, for equality, for what is good and honorable, right and true.

Questions for Contemplation:
Turning Inward:
How have you risen above difficult times in your life?
Turning Outward:
What creative work can you do in the world to help empower others to rise, as well?

Tiamat/Tehom

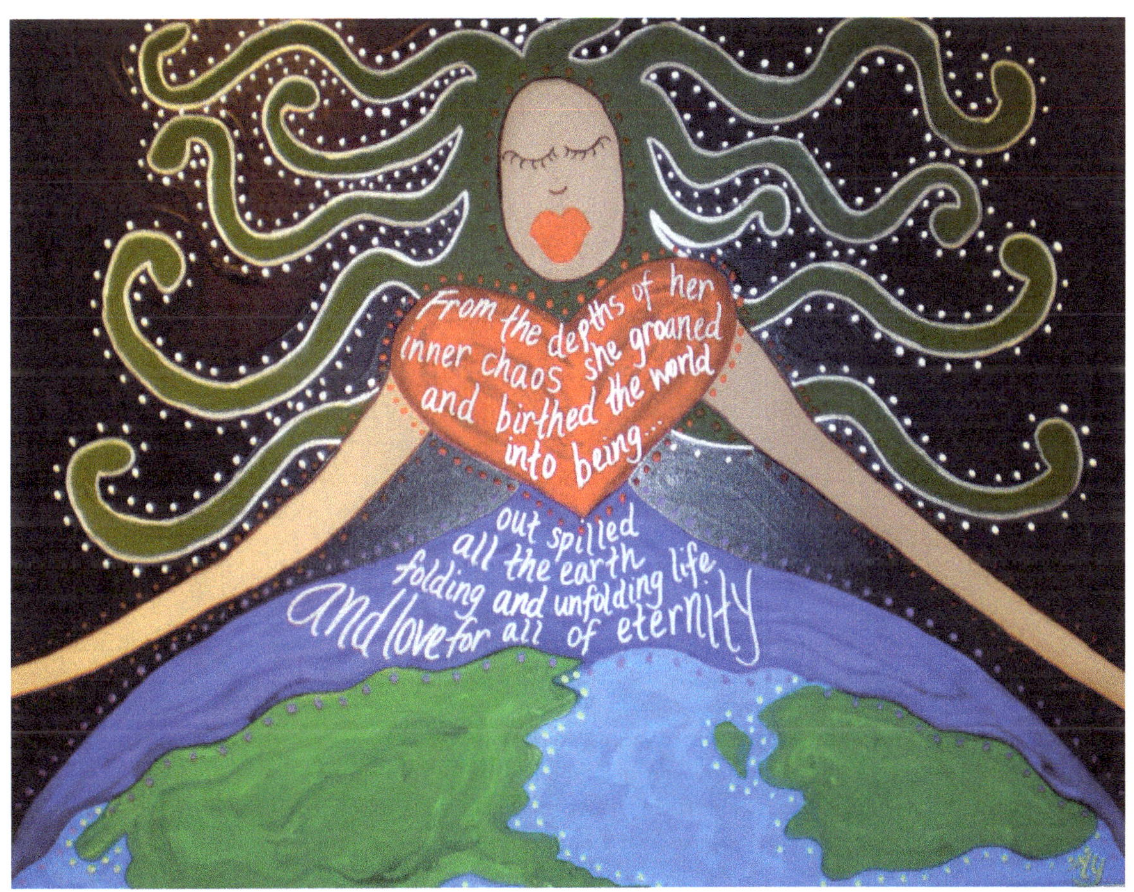

Tiamat/Tehem
Acrylic on Canvas, 16x20, Garber Private Collection

Tiamat/Tehom

In Genesis 1 we read, "In beginning, God created the heavens and the earth, the earth was a formless void and darkness covered the face of the deep, while a wind from God swept over the face of the waters." It is the creation narrative held dear, formative, and meaningful for countless Jews and Christians. Interestingly, this word, deep, in Hebrew is *tehom. Tehom* translates as "deep or depths," but it's also a cognate for Tiamat, a Babylonian Goddess of creation. Out of the face of the deep, the world begins. Out of *tehom*, God creates. Out of Tiamat, the earth comes into being. This dancing Babylonian goddess syncretistically intermingles with the creation myth so pivotal to the faith of Christians and Jews in a way that could be terrifying, or beautiful, or—like the chaotic body of Tiamat that brings the world into being—both.

Catherine Keller deconstructs the terror therein and constructs the potentially parodied and subversive beauty of this esoteric cognate in her book, *Face of the Deep: A Theology of Becoming*. My interest in this earth goddess piqued while traveling the Middle East and witnessing carvings of her dancing body: eyes filled with rage, arms outstretched to protect her children, healing snakes spilling out of the folds of her skirt, her distended body splitting open so that earth and life and all creation could be and become. It haunted me. And then I read Keller. Most of my interpretation and artistic choices rely on her beautiful work.

Keller recounts the way the Babylonian myth, the *Enuma Elish*, portrays Tiamat as the ever-raging sea monster mother who must be slain by her own child, Marduk, the might warrior who prevails uncensored. Before the war-hungry myth demonized Tiamat, however, she was regarded as the mother of all humanity, all creation, the one who births the world into being. Keller asks, "How does a religion manage to vilify the goddess it still recognizes as cosmic parent of all that is (Catherine Keller, *Face of the Deep*, 28)?" The creation in the *Enuma Elish*, in an incredibly abbreviated form, goes like this.

Tiamat and her primal mate, Apsu, create children. Apsu finds the children too noisy and has a difficult time resting. He wants to destroy the children so he can sleep. Tiamat rages furiously (rightly so, most mothers would add). Apsu calls on the second generation to help with his plans. Tiamat grows so furious and restless that she begins to breed monsters. Marduk, her own child, emerges as the soon-to-be great warrior who will slaughter her. Marduk creates *imhullu*, an evil wind, and lets the evil wind loose in her face. Because her mouth is open in a scream, she ingests the wind, it fills her belly, distending it a deadly parody of pregnancy. As she opens her mouth wide, Marduk shoots an arrow between her lips and it tears Tiamat apart. He then constructs "the cosmos from her oceanic carcass (Keller, 107)."

She who gave birth to them all becomes the martyr for their continued existence. Out of her slaughtered body becomes all that is. The narrative turns the concept of *creation ex nihilo* on its head, the formless void that is its empty and thoughtless head. There are some striking similarities that give us pause. The formless void, in Hebrew *tovo va bohu* may well refer to Tiamat's slain body. Some claim that the "wind from God"—*ruah* in Hebrew—that swept across the face of the deep is the *imhullu* used by Marduk to slay Tiamat. Keller reminds us, however, that the *ruah* (God's spirit or breath) of the Hebrew bible is never viewed as evil, but as life-giving, life-forming, feminine, and good. Tiamat and *tehom* are both feminine words. And so is *ruah*.

Keller claims that the evocation of Tiamat, embedded in the Hebrew *tehom*, indicates a crafty parody of the Babylonian creation from chaos. Her insights are worth recounting at length:

> In Tiamat's "heart-pondering," may we not receive a clue for a hermeneutics that would let her live: her, the primal creativity, where children run wild, where the new is granted a costly permission by its antecedents; the body of all that is silenced or slaughtered so that the new order need not negotiate its claim? Such a tehomic hermeneutic, haunted by the dead goddess but not worshiping her, would not find the chaos waters always pacific. It would tune its texts to a universe that puts up with a lot of painful noise. It would teach its insecure traditions that turbulence, though it may have ill effects, cannot be excluded without murder…If we read the layered deep of Genesis 1.2 as a cunning parody of the Babylonian creation from chaos, we might regain the peacemaking Tiamat and expose the warrior. He has occupied the Abrahamic traditions in her absence (Keller, 122).

Who knew that embedded in the traditions that have often forsaken women, using this same creation narrative from Genesis to marginalize and oppress them, was this brave and wild goddess? Who knew that lurking within the creation story Jews and Christians cling to, claiming dominion over this chaotic earth, was the Babylonian earth goddess Tiamat? Interestingly, Keller offers a slight critique, or at least a need for expansion, in the heteronormative dalliances of the female Tiamat and male Apsu. But a queer reading of Genesis 1 might do the subverting for us.
The masculine *imhulu* wind may have "impregnated" Tiamat in the Babylonian narrative, but the wind from God—*ruah*—that sweeps over the face of the deep, the face of Tiamat, is also feminine. In these ways, the sexual imagery is female and female. Out of this chaotic and windy union of two feminine beings, the world springs forth. Hetero-dalliances are nowhere to be found. Instead, it is the folding and unfolding of the feminine chaos between Tiamat/*tehom* and *ruah* that birth the world.

Keller states that tehomic love means that "to love is to bear with the chaos (Keller, 29)." Bearing with this churning chaos, Tiamat teaches us that much lies beneath the surface of a text if one does not implore a deeper reading, a reading of the depths. So, out of Tiamat's oceanic womb, the earth is in the process of being born in my icon. As I canonize Tiamat into holiness, her protective arms spread wide, covering all the earth, and all her children therein. Her hair flies wildly and her heart cries out to us:

From the depths of her inner chaos
She groaned
And birthed the world into being…
Out spilled all the earth
Folding and unfolding life and love
For all eternity

Not only does Tiamat teach us that much lies beneath the surface, hidden in the folds, washed over by the very breath of god(dess). She also reminds us that life and love and flourishing dwells, not outside of chaos, not by conquering chaos, but within chaos. "The answers are out there in the drowning deep," the singer Vienna Tang reminds us. In the womb of the earth, in the salty waters of chaos, in the drowning deep, we find life and love and eternity. Forever.

Questions for Contemplation:
Turning Inward:
How might you find inspiration within the chaos of your life?
Turning Outward:
How might you help create beauty and wonder amidst the chaos of other's lives?

Holy Women Icons: Commissions and Gifts

Thus far, we have explored the stories of holy women that are well-known, perhaps not by the wider public, but by feminists seeking to uncover the forgotten truths of holy women throughout history. They are goddesses, saints, artists, dancers, scholars, clergy, and pillars of the faith. We tell their stories in our classrooms. Their stories embolden us to stay strong, and continue working for justice and equality. But what of the women whose songs really are unsung, whose stories never grace the pages of our textbooks? What about the women who have, indeed, emboldened us, paved the way for us to be who we are, but who most people have never heard of? Many such women are also holy, thus deserving of canonization as a Holy Woman Icon.

In her foundational work that highlights the importance of telling women's stories, Carol Christ begins by saying:

> Women's stories have not been told. And without stories there is no articulation of experience. Without stories a woman is lost when she comes to make the important decisions of her life. She does not learn to value her struggles, to celebrate her strengths, to comprehend her pain. Without stories she cannot understand herself. Without stories she is alienated from those experiences of self and world that have been called spiritual or religious. She is closed in silence. The expression of women's spiritual quest is integrally related to the telling of women's stories. If women's stories are not told, the depth of women's souls will not be known. (Carol Christ, *Diving Deep and Surfacing: Women Writers on Spiritual Quest*, 1)

I would like to contend, like Christ, that the telling of women's stories is important. This is why I paint my Holy Women Icons, canonizing their lives and beings with a brush stroke, deeming these myriad revolutionary women "holy" by virtue of painting them as icons. But it is not only these seemingly famous women—these heroines of feminism—who are holy and whose stories matter. It is also those unknown mothers, courageous sisters, daring daughters, and bold lovers who make our world a more just and holy place. As such, I would like for you to know about some of these women. On the pages that follow, more Holy Women Icons spill forth, their hearts crying out to us. Some of these women have commissioned an icon for themselves as a reminder of who they want to be and become. Others had a personal icon commissioned on their behalf to celebrate an important day: ordinations, births, graduations. Others inspired me so that I created their icon as a gift of gratitude for the beauty of their lives and the way they have emboldened and inspired me. All are holy. In glimpsing briefly at their lives, witnessing their holiness, I hope that you will also realize your own innate holiness.

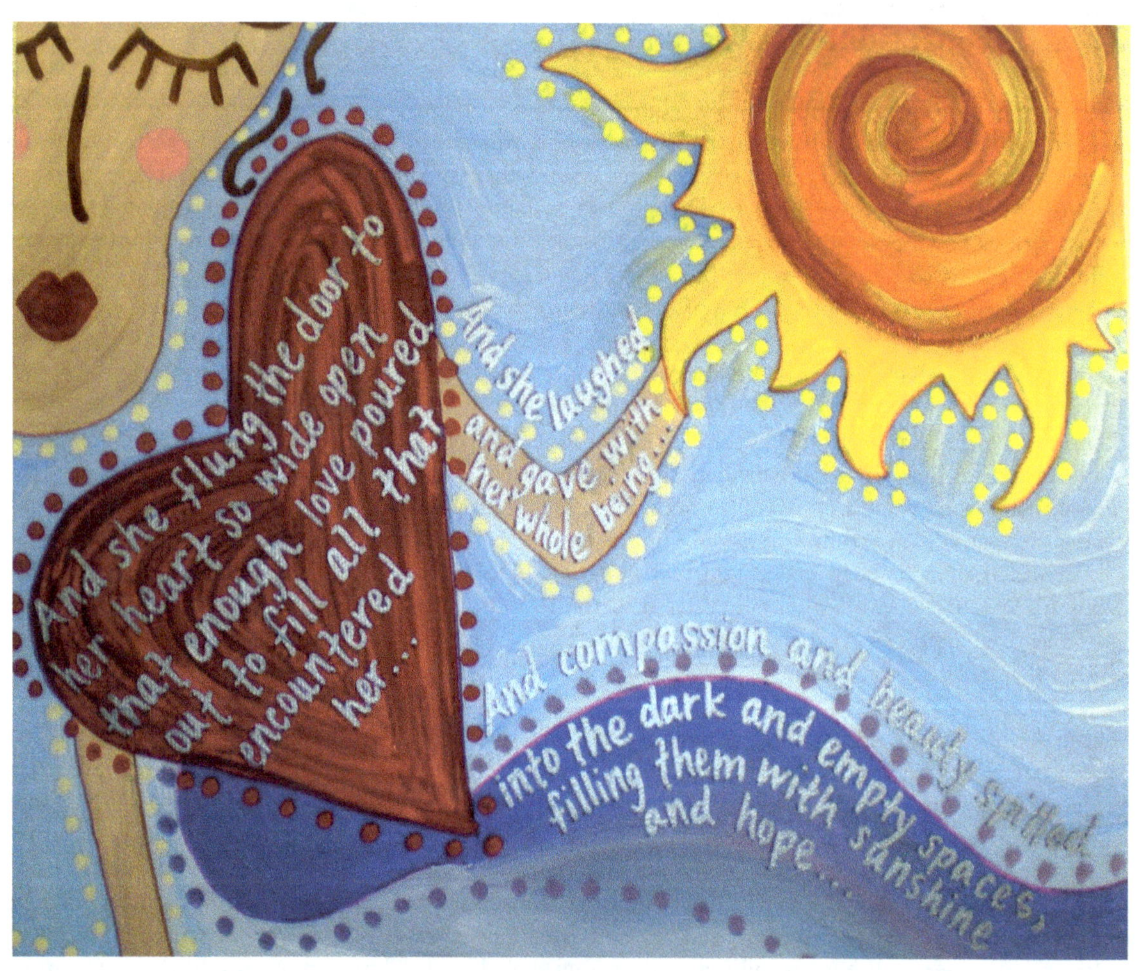

Elizabeth
Acrylic on Canvas, 12x12, Lee Private Collection
My beautiful, brilliant, compassionate wife

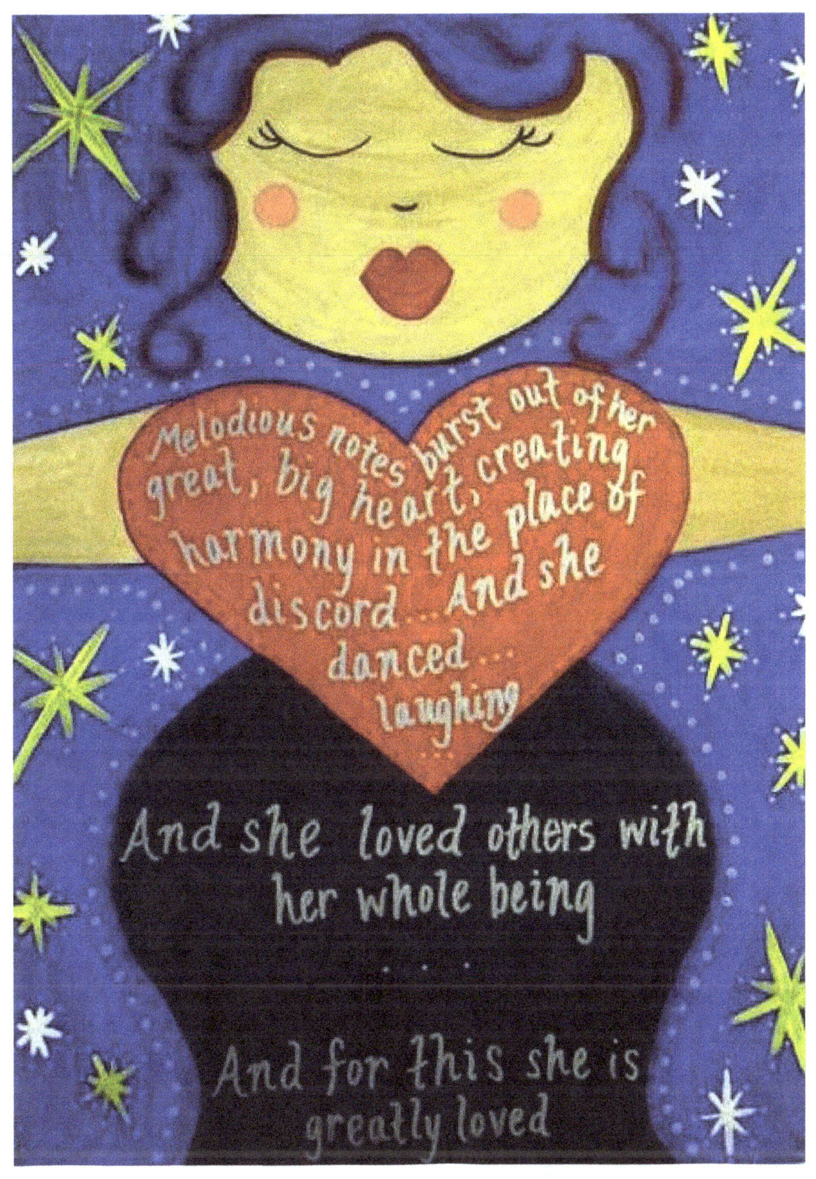

Mary
Acrylic on Canvas, 12x16, Harrell Private Collection
My mother

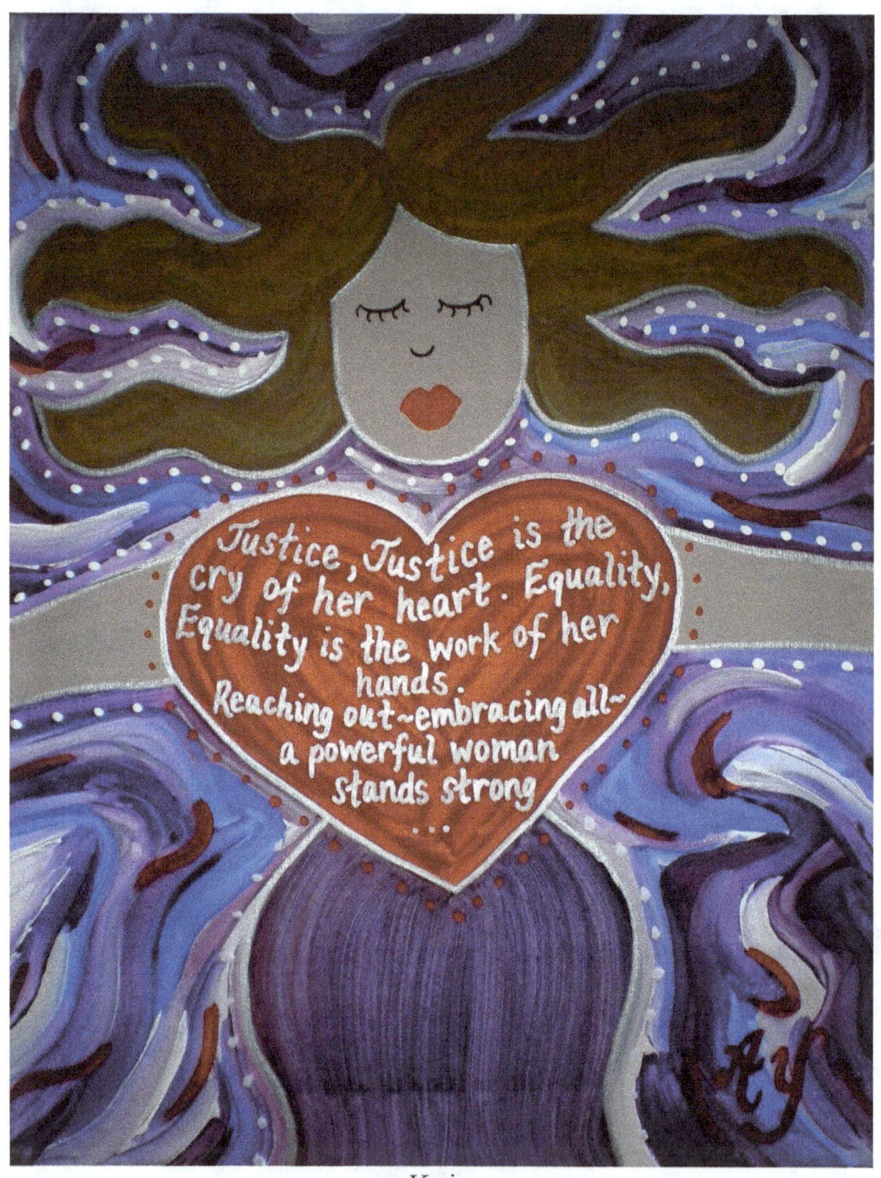

Katie
Acrylic on Canvas, 12x16, Fowler Private Collection
Commissioned for an attorney who works for justice

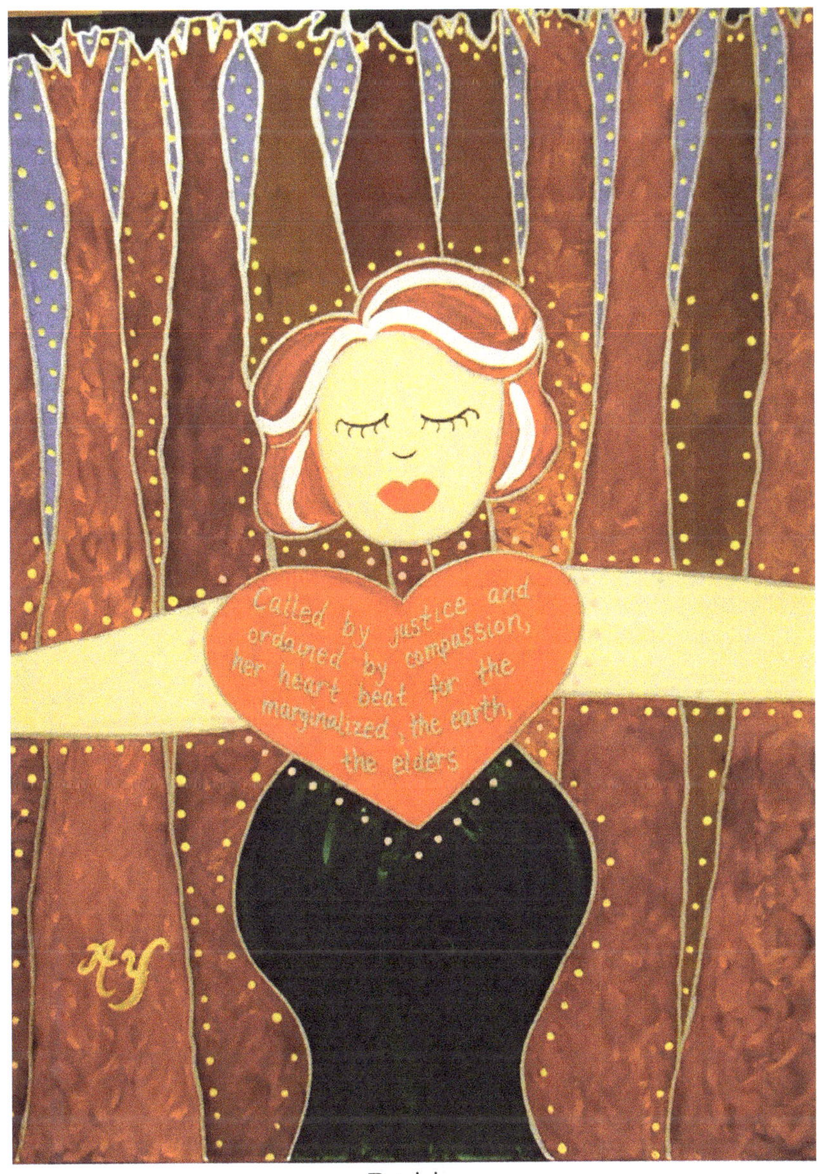

Patricia
Acrylic on Canvas, 16x20, Wood Private Collection
Commissioned by a minister among the redwoods upon her ordination

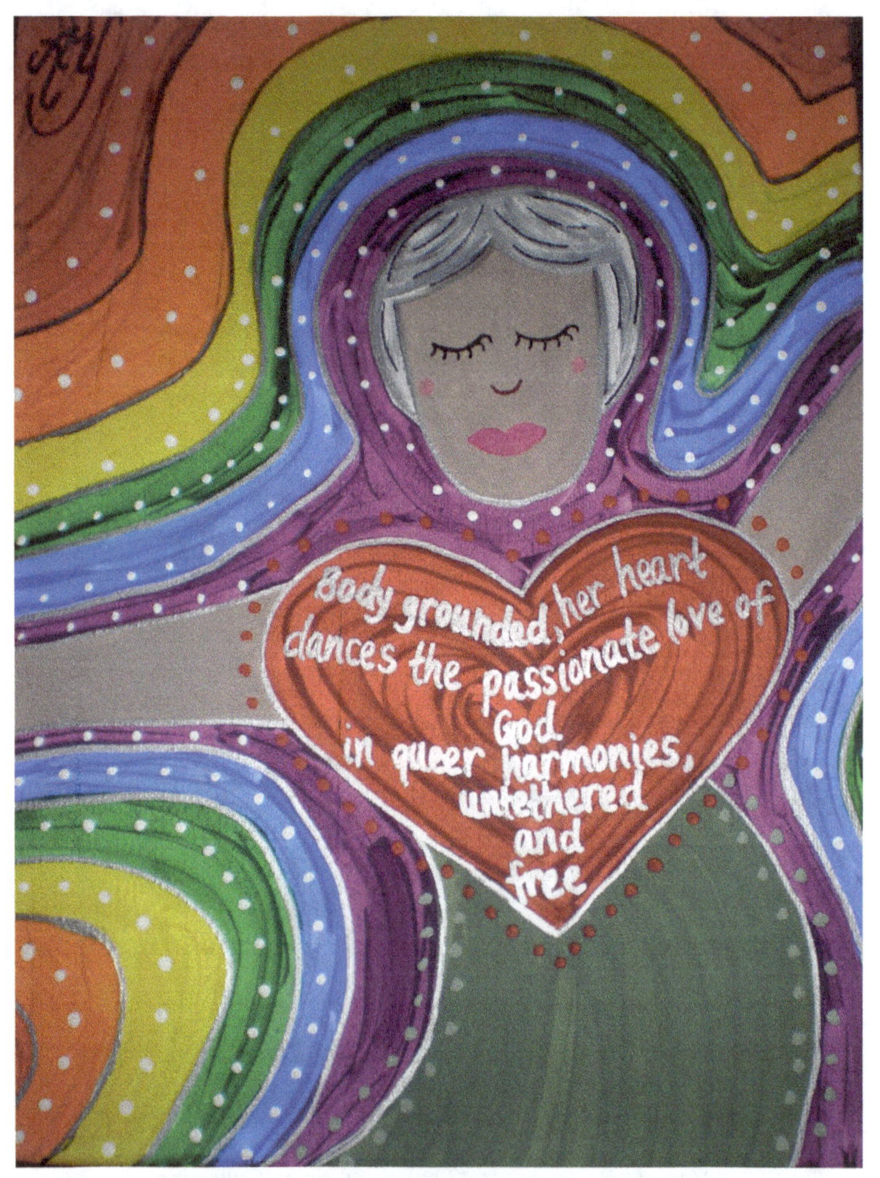

Kittredge
Acrylic on Canvas, 12x16, Cherry Private Collection
Commission for LGBTQ activist and author; words by Cherry

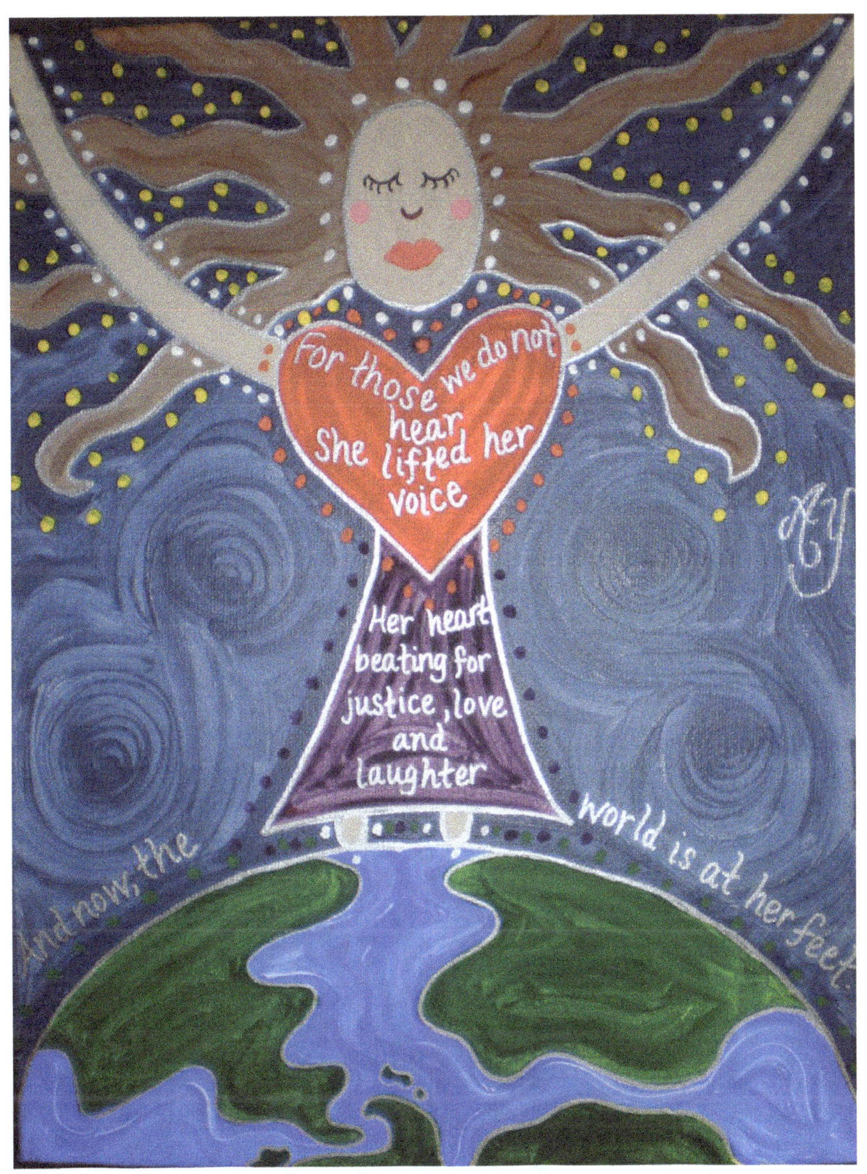

Katy
Acrylic on Canvas, 12x16, Duran Private Collection
Commission upon the graduation of an amazing young woman and ally

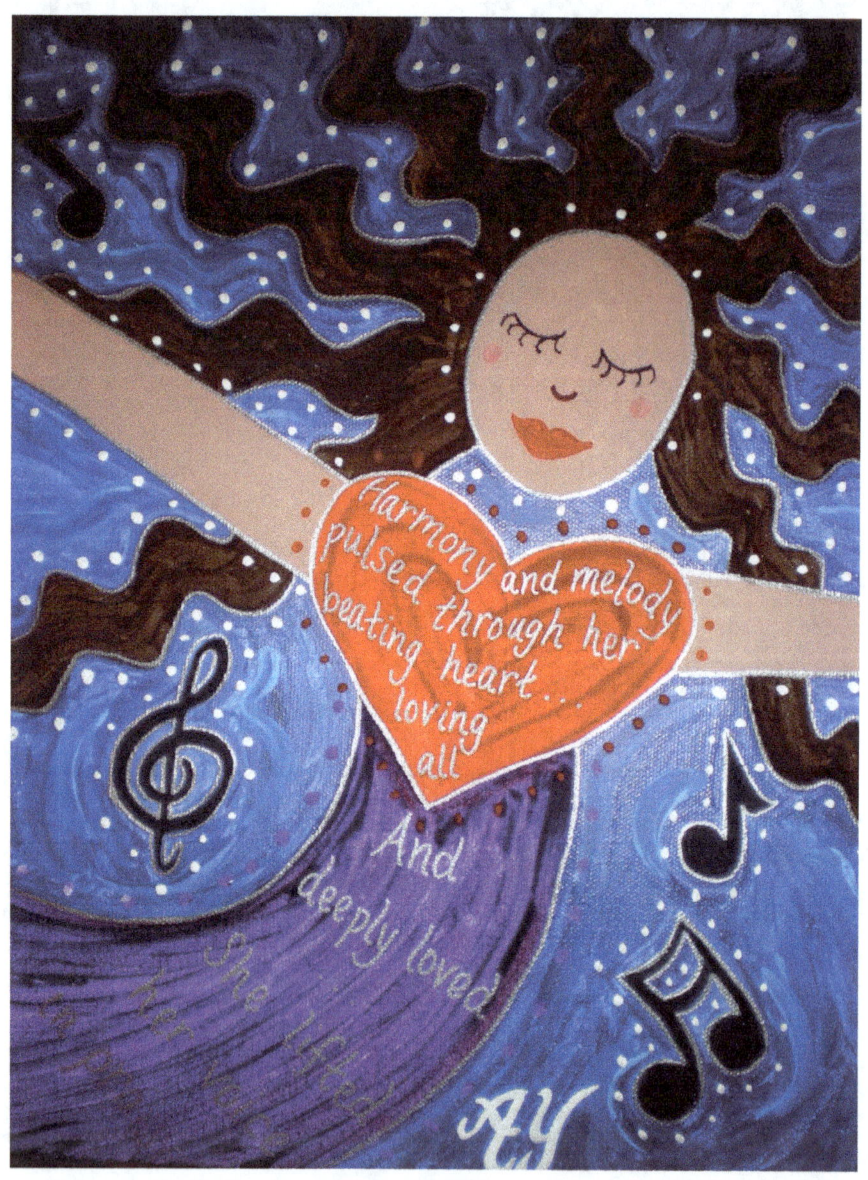

Jen
Acrylic on Canvas, 12x16, Van Camp Private Collection
Commission for a gifted musician and thoughtful youth minister

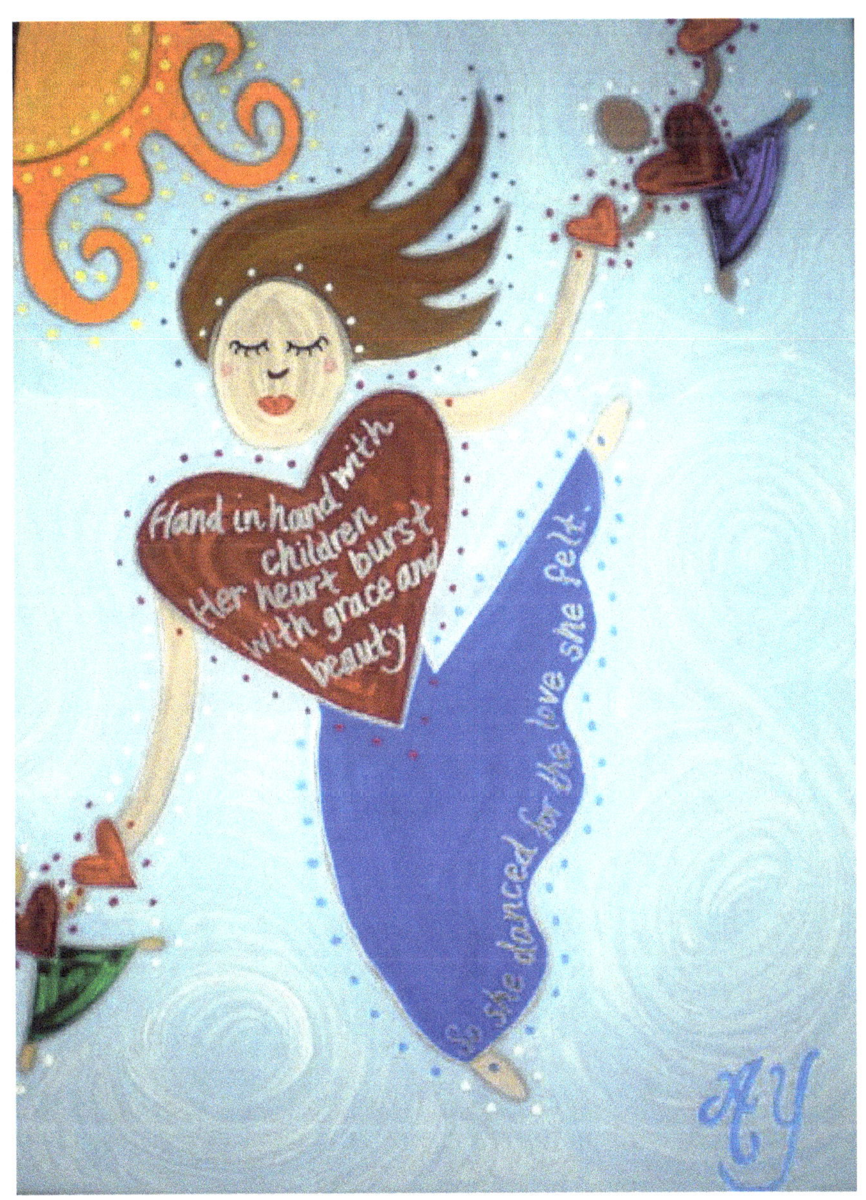

Rebecca
Acrylic on Canvas; 16x20; Orton Private Collection
Commission for a dancer and children's minister

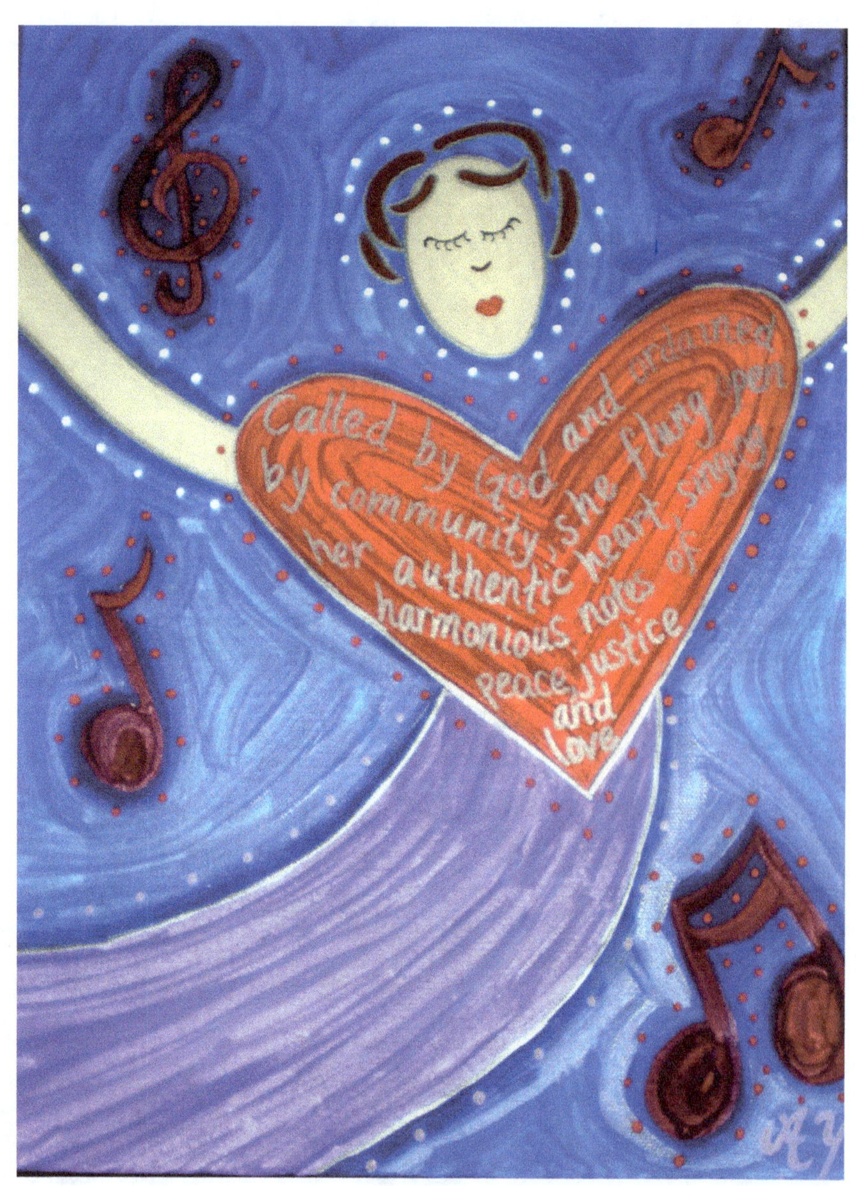

Jodie
Acrylic on Canvas; 12x16; Tooley Private Collection
Ordination gift for an authentic and talented clergywoman

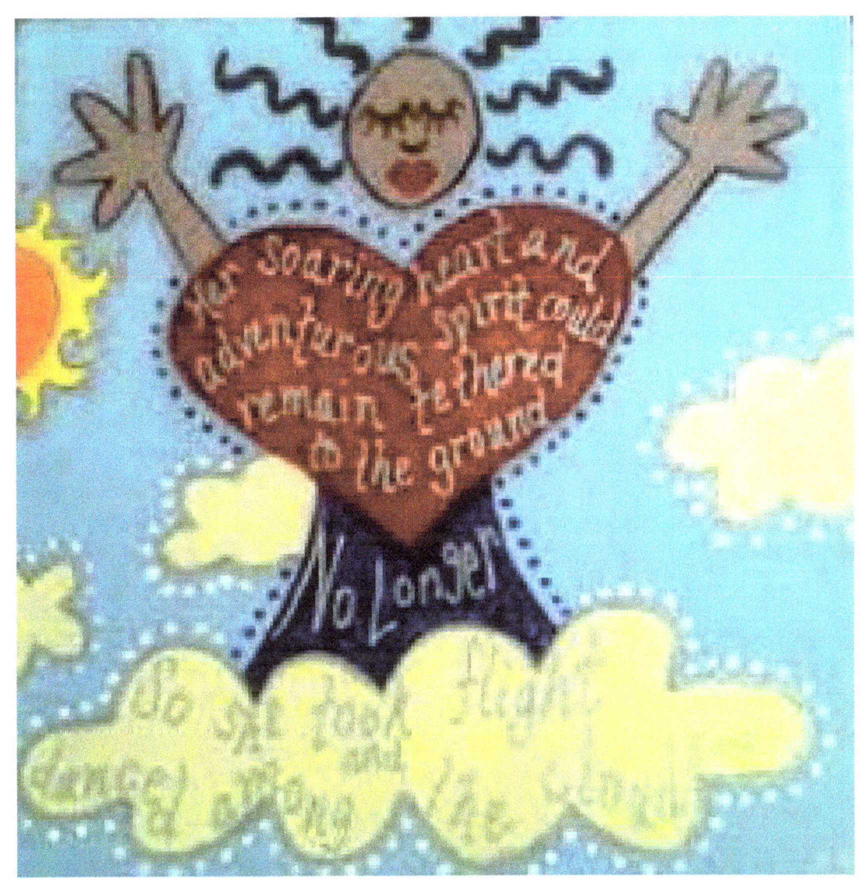

Margaret
Acrylic on Canvas; 12x12; Harrell Private Collection
My aunt, the world's greatest flight attendant

Questions for Contemplation:
Turning Inward:
What are the most holy and inspirational parts of your own heart? How are you a Holy Woman Icon?
Turning Outward:
Who are the Holy Women Icons in your life? How can you honor their legacy?

www.ingramcontent.com/pod-product-compliance
Lightning Source LLC
LaVergne TN
LVHW080322110826
845155LV00026B/182